Targeting Zero

Embodied and Whole Life Carbon explained

RIBA Publishing

© RIBA Publishing, 2017

Published by RIBA Publishing, part of RIBA Enterprises Ltd, The Old Post Office,
St Nicholas Street, Newcastle upon Tyne, NE1 1RH

ISBN 978-1-85946-643-8 / 978-1-85946-816-6 (PDF)

The right of Simon Sturgis to be identified as the Author of this Work has been
asserted in accordance with the Copyright, Designs and Patents Act 1988
sections 77 and 78.

British Library Cataloguing-in-Publication Data
A catalogue record for this book is available from the British Library.

Commissioning Editor: Elizabeth Webster
Production: Richard Blackburn
Designed & Typeset by Ashley Western
Printed and bound by Page Bros, Norwich, UK
Cover designed by Kneath Associates
Cover image credits: Shutterstock: www.shutterstock.com

While every effort has been made to check the accuracy and quality of the
information given in this publication, neither the Author nor the Publisher
accept any responsibility for the subsequent use of this information, for any
errors or omissions that it may contain, or for any misunderstandings arising
from it.

www.ribaenterprises.com

C

CONTENTS

Contents

A
ACKNOWLEDGEMENTS

For Victoria

Acknowledgements

The writing of this book owes a lot to many people. I would like to thank those with whom I have worked over the last few years at SCP, without whose contributions this book would not exist. In particular I would like to thank Gareth Roberts for a great collaboration and for his original thinking that helped get these ideas started; Qian Li for making things happen; Juan Lafuente for amazing insights; Elizabeth Common for endless support; Mirko Farnetani and Juan Lafuente for their work on the graphics in this book; Athina Papakosta for the technical review of the section 'Implementing the British Standard: BS EN 15978'; and Maiia Williams, Andrea Carvajal, Sara Godinho, Priyanka Arora, Myrtia Fasouli, Theo Darviris, Olga Koumaditou, Leo Cheung, James Robb, Martina Arata and Christina Stuart for contributing to the thinking within this book.

I would also like to thank those who have shown confidence in and support for me personally in this field over the last ten years: Paul Morrell OBE, Lynne Sullivan OBE, John Connaughton, Paul Finch, Hattie Hartman, Sarah Cary, Victoria Herring, Thomas Lane, Neil Pennell and Peter Runacres.

Making sense of the complex world of carbon

In 2008, we invited Simon Sturgis to speak at the inaugural World Architecture Festival in Barcelona about the relationship of embodied carbon to operational carbon in respect of buildings: the traditional notion that operational emissions were all that mattered was exposed as a myth. Energy analysis at the time was a blunt instrument, focusing on performance over construction and the production of materials and components. Simon not only showed this as a flawed approach, but also offered propositions for optimisation strategies to limit carbon generation over time.

A while later, a Technology Strategy Board discussion about carbon included a message that retrofitting of buildings needed to be promoted and celebrated in the public arena and In 2010 the Architects' Journal launched its Retrofit Awards, benefiting from Simon's support and advice as a long-standing judge. He is an admirable hybrid: a green (with a small 'g') activist and an architect with a profound interest in science and technology. The creation of his carbon consultancy SCP has seen a steady flow of research and proposition, all based on real-world analysis and scenarios, in which tricky territories have been opened up for holistic examination.

This book is a summary of much of that work. It has the passion of a manifesto, but avoids doctrinaire instructions. Much of the advice, which derives from case studies and measurement, should be taken up by anyone involved in significant construction activity. Carbon analysis needs to be understood in the round; it needs to embrace lifetime change (maintenance, repair, renewal) not just short-term outputs; it needs to acknowledge the changing relationship between embodied carbon and operational carbon emissions over time. It also needs to take into account the final stage of the life of most buildings: the most wasteful (demolition); a better option (recycling); or the best option (re-use).

The aspirations expressed in these pages are in the spirit of phrase, coined by RIBA president Sir Alex Gordon, that buildings should be `long life, loose fit, low energy'. This book re-interprets that clarion call, arguing for maximum life, maximum flexibility, maximum re-use and as close to zero carbon as we can get.

Paul Finch
Paul Finch is programme director of the World Architecture Festival and editorial director of the Architects' Journal

F

FOREWORD

We live in an era of unprecedented scientific and technological discovery, yet paradoxically, we also find ourselves confronted with humanity's greatest challenge: a planet that cannot replenish its resources, and a rapidly warming atmosphere that's threatening multiple life forms due to fossil fuel burning and man-made greenhouse gas emissions.

The good news is that governments, businesses and citizens around the world have woken up to climate change, agreeing to transition to a very low carbon economy within the next thirty years. The challenge, however, is the speed of that transition.

Buildings are essential for the survival of humanity, but are also responsible for a staggering 30% of the world's carbon emissions. This figure doesn't include transport emissions or the industrial processes associated with product manufacture. So anyone serious about eliminating the climate change impact of the built environment must take seriously the notion of reducing whole-life carbon emissions.

UK Green Building Council's (UK-GBC) vision is of a built environment that is fully decarbonised. As such, we will continue to advocate for embodied carbon to become a mainstream issue in building design, construction and maintenance. We believe that sustainable development must become second nature to the built environment industry. This will require carbon literacy, accounting and management to underpin every decision. Carbon is a currency we all need to be comfortable dealing in. Yet embodied carbon remains an elusive concept to even the most dedicated sustainability professionals – let alone the millions of built environment practitioners shaping our urban fabric every day.

It is high time that practical and comprehensive books such as this appear on the essential reading list of practitioners worldwide. Having worked closely with Simon Sturgis and his team on the refurbishment of the UK-GBC's own headquarters in London during 2016, we were thrilled to achieve the lowest embodied carbon footprint of an office refit ever recorded in the UK. This can only be achieved through a meticulously rigorous and relentless focus on the carbon implications of every decision along the way – as exemplified in this book, through the calculation of embodied carbon at every stage in the RIBA lifecycle.

There is now no excuse to avoid taking corrective action. The clock is ticking on climate change, and with books such as this, we can equip ourselves with the knowledge and solutions to overcome. So let's get on with it.

Julie Hirigoyen *CEO of UK-GBC*

Introduction

In 2010 the Royal Institute of Chartered Surveyors (RICS) published 'Redefining Zero',[1] which explored moving on from a purely operational energy assessment of buildings towards a 'whole life' approach to carbon assessment. In particular, this paper highlighted the fact that carbon emissions from making, maintaining and repairing buildings constitute a significant proportion of a building's lifetime emissions.

This book, *Targeting Zero,* follows on from *Redefining Zero* with the aim of explaining a practical approach to carbon emissions reduction in the built environment. It is focused around the work and experience of the consultancy Sturgis Carbon Profiling LLP (SCP). SCP has been working on material-related carbon emissions analysis since 2007. SCP's work has been wide-ranging in terms of project types – from new-build owner/occupier offices to Georgian residential retrofit – and in terms of scale: from construction projects with a value of more than £800m down to the carbon footprint of coffee. This book shares our experience in this increasingly important area.

Targeting Zero is written around a selection of practical case studies, all of which examine ways to reduce embodied and whole life carbon emissions. It is worth noting that we are still learning how best to assess and deliver resource-efficient low carbon outcomes.

The title of this book highlights the fact that while zero emissions may be the aim, as a society we have some considerable distance to go before a truly zero carbon building can be achieved. It is the author's view that the current use of the words 'zero carbon', which refers to operational emissions only, is incorrect and misleading as there are very few buildings (generally basic, primitive or simple dwellings) that make no carbon impact on the environment. For today's society, with its complex construction methodologies, a truly zero carbon building is simply not possible, and offsetting only masks the issue. However, that does not mean it should not remain a utopian aspiration: one that we target, even if unattainable.

A principal aim of this book is to show from practical experience how to reduce carbon footprint through the construction and use of buildings. This means reducing both the use of fossil fuels and the creation of greenhouse gases. Reducing fossil fuel use started when the 1970s oil crisis brought a stop to cheap energy. Oil became an economic weapon, and the stage was set for today's energy-related legislation. There were a series of energy crises between 1967 and 1979, caused by problems in the Middle East, but the most significant began as a result of Arab oil producers imposing an embargo in 1973.

The decision to boycott America and punish the west in response to support for Israel in the Yom Kippur War against Egypt led the price of crude to rise from $3 per barrel to $12 by 1974.[2]

In 1965 the required U-value for walls was 1.7. In 1976 as a result of the 1973 oil crisis, building regulations reduced the required U-value down to 1.[3]

Now, however, the emphasis has shifted as climate change and resource depletion have become increasingly important. These are identified by the Ministry of Defence as two of the five strategic challenges facing the UK. The other three are inequality, population growth and the shift of power from west to east.[4] The UK's low carbon transition plan[5] makes it a legal requirement for the UK to achieve an 80% reduction of emissions from 1990 levels by 2050. For the built environment industry, this cannot be achieved purely by encouraging reduced energy use in buildings. Achieving material-related carbon emissions reductions, and improving the efficiency with which materials are used, is of vital importance. *The Carbon Crunch* by Dieter Helm[6] notes that a prime reason for the UK's recent emissions reductions is simply that manufacturing has been outsourced to other countries. To achieve real change, it is essential that we reduce our demand for high carbon products.

The built environment in all its forms is essential for the survival of humanity. Paradoxically, the decisions we take over how we make and use this environment are starting to contribute to our destruction, principally through climate change and depletion of resources. Those in the built environment industry have a particular opportunity and, indeed, responsibility to evolve ways of reducing environmental damage resulting from the construction and use of buildings.

The carbon emissions impacts of constructing and maintaining buildings over their lifetimes are increasingly significant due to the success of the Building Regulations and BREEAM in reducing operational energy usage. In most new building types, lifetime embodied carbon emissions can now exceed the regulated operational emissions from day-to-day energy use. Material-related or 'embodied' carbon emissions are therefore crucial in making further progress (see Chapter 1).

Through better-informed design choices, architects and designers can directly reduce many of these emissions, and can also help to change the thinking and culture around the use of buildings and structures. Reducing embodied carbon emissions, and the associated resource efficiency involved, will not only profoundly change the way buildings are designed but will also have further implications for architecture and the environment in which it exists.

Huge strides have been made in operational energy reduction, to the point where buildings today use considerably less energy than even 20 years ago. Further such reductions remain important to overall carbon emissions reduction, but they are becoming increasingly difficult to achieve cheaply and in quantity. The problem with current legislation is that it encourages actions to reduce operational carbon emissions without regard for the embodied carbon consequences. An example would be disregarding the carbon emissions cost of covering a building in louvres in favour of the carbon emissions benefit of reduced heating loads. Taking a holistic or a whole life view of carbon emissions is critical to optimising carbon emissions reduction in the built environment.

Taking a more holistic approach to low carbon design will enable architects and structural engineers to play an increasingly key role in determining the whole life carbon footprint of the buildings they design. It will shift the responsibility for carbon emissions reduction from the services engineer to the architect. An important part of this is life cycle analysis (LCA). LCAs are discussed in Chapter 6 (see also ISOs 14040 and 14044)[7] but, in summary, an LCA examines, at the design stage, a building's anticipated fabric and energy performance over its projected lifespan. This means that, to achieve low carbon outcomes, building designers need to think long-term from the outset.

The work of all practitioners and consultants in the field of carbon emissions reduction is in accordance with the European Standard CEN TC 350,[8] incorporated into the British Standard BS EN 15978:2011[9] (and including BS EN 15804).[10] It is worth noting at the outset that, while this is a sensible starting point, it is proving difficult to implement with consistency.

Practical experience of BS EN 15978 has identified several problems with respect to carbon analysis and reporting:

- Different consultants implement the standard in different ways, giving rise to divergent assessments of the same building types.

- There are a number of issues – such as whether or not to include grid decarbonisation, and to what level – that are not clear from the Standard.

- Different clients require different levels of reporting, and to differing levels of detail, meaning that similar buildings cannot properly be compared.

There is, however, significant and increasing demand for consistent embodied and whole life carbon reporting, not just from client bodies but also local authorities, and anyone who wishes to report under Scope 3 emissions in the fullest possible way.

In 2015, the Department for Business Innovation and Skills funding arm InnovateUK (formerly the Technology Strategy Board) provided funding for an industry-wide team to produce an implementation plan for making BS EN 15978 consistent and understandable in use, and usable and accessible through the RICS certification as a 'professional statement'.[11] The implementation plan also calls for compatibility with BIM and BREEAM 2018. The successful rollout of this project (Implementing Whole Life Carbon in Buildings [IWLCIB]) will provide a benchmark consistent with EU and British Standards to enable consultants, property companies, public bodies, local authorities and software designers to work to a common set of parameters. This project completes in mid-2017.

Assuming RICS and BREEAM definition and integration, embodied and whole life carbon analysis and reporting should become mainstream. This will ensure a reliable template for whole life carbon emissions reduction. This book therefore represents a summary of where things are today.

While this book focuses on carbon emissions, there are other important considerations for designing for better buildings generally, such as wellbeing and health. For example, the International Living Future Institute in Seattle produces the Living Building Challenge,[12] a performance standard that uses a range of more 'human' metrics, including the Healthy Materials Red List, which identifies material toxicity. The International WELL Building Institute also uses similar health and wellbeing metrics.

This book is not a textbook in the more severe sense but is aimed at informing architects, engineers, contractors and clients who wish to understand this topic better through the practical experience of one practitioner. I hope you find it useful.

All case studies are by SCP from live projects.

*To undertake or commission a whole life carbon assessment, it is recommended that you focus on **Chapter 2**, specifically the section **Reducing embodied and whole life carbon through the RIBA work stages**, together with **Chapter 6**, specifically the section **Implementing the British Standard BS EN 15978**.*

1

Embodied, operational and whole life carbon

Overview

Carbon emissions from the creation of the built environment derive principally from energy used in the construction process. This largely means energy generated from fossil fuels, ie coal, oil and gas. Energy supplied from renewable sources, nuclear power and hydroelectric power does not generally produce direct operational carbon emissions. (It is, however, worth noting that the process of building, for example, wind turbines consumes a significant amount of energy, so the provision of wind power is not totally free of carbon emissions.)

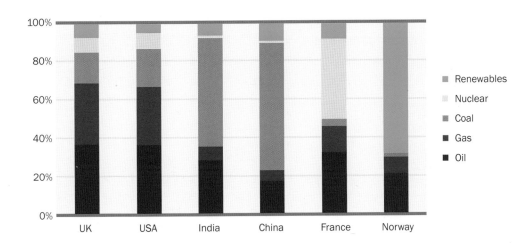

Figure 1.01: Global energy consumption by country in 2014: six examples.

Currently in the UK, and for the medium term at least, reducing carbon emissions is substantially about reducing energy use. Buildings use energy to operate, known as 'operational energy', which produces 'operational carbon emissions'.

Sourcing materials, constructing, repairing and maintaining buildings are also responsible for significant energy use – this is referred to as 'embodied energy', giving rise to the term 'embodied carbon emissions'. The country from which your materials are sourced – ie under which sort of energy regimes they are extracted and fabricated – will have an impact on the carbon footprint of that material. Electricity used by industry in the UK is generally from a mix of sources; sourcing outside the UK can open up opportunities for procuring low carbon materials – but a word of caution: transport methods to a UK site can counteract these benefits.

'Whole life carbon emissions' are both the operational and the embodied emissions considered together over the life of the building. A key point is that considering operational or embodied emissions in isolation can lead to poor decision-making with unintended consequences.

The terms 'carbon' or 'carbon emissions' as used in this book actually refer to 'carbon dioxide emissions and their equivalents', or CO_2e, where the 'e' refers to a bundle of greenhouse gases (GHGs) that have similar negative impacts to CO_2 but at a significantly worse level per kg of the gas.

Gas	Chemical formula	Lifetime (years)	Global warming potential (GWP) for given time horizon		
			20 years	100 years	500 years
Carbon dioxide	CO_2	30-95	1	1	1
Methane	CH_4	12	72	25	7.6
Nitrous oxide	N_2O	114	289	298	153
CFC-12	CCl_2F_2	100	11,000	10,900	5,200
HCFC-22	$CHClF_2$	12	5,160	1,810	549
Tetrafluoromethane	CF_4	50,000	5,210	7,390	11,200
Hexafluoroethane	C_2F_6	10,000	8,630	12,200	18,200
Sulphur hexafluoride	SF_6	3,200	16,300	22,800	32,600
Nitrogen trifluoride	NF_3	740	12,300	17,200	20,700

Table 1.01: Atmospheric lifetime and global warming potential relative to CO_2 at different time horizons for various greenhouse gases. Note that a number of these gases are constituents of fabrication processes; for example, some glues used in making laminated timber structure. This can increase the CO_2e footprint of what is perceived as a 'green' material to a point where it is a poor environmental performer.
Source: SCP with data from IPCC (2007)**

Legislative background – the short story

The European Committee for Standardization, known as CEN, has technical committees (TCs) that produce standards on a whole range of activities and processes for use across the EU. The one that concerns us for carbon emissions reduction is CEN/TC 350, the standard for sustainability of construction works, produced in 2005.

In addition to CEN/TC 350 is the UK Low Carbon Transition Plan: National strategy for climate and energy, presented to Parliament by the government on 15 July 2009. For our purposes, the key extract from the 'five point plan' is item four:

> ### 4. Building a low carbon UK
> To play our part in reducing global emissions, Britain needs to become a low carbon country. The 2008 Climate Change Act[1] made Britain the first country in the world to set legally binding 'carbon budgets', aiming to cut UK emissions by 34% by 2020 and at least 80% by 2050 through investment in energy efficiency and clean energy technologies such as renewables, nuclear and carbon capture and storage.[2]

This document focuses principally on reducing operational energy use in buildings, but not embodied energy; nor did it consider the possible implications of pursuing an operational energy-only approach.

However, in the autumn of 2010, The UK Department of Business Innovation and Skills' innovation and growth team (IGT), under the direction of the government's chief construction advisor, Paul Morrell (formally senior partner of Davis Langdon), produced its final report on low carbon construction. This excellent document posed the question 'Is the construction industry fit for purpose for the transition to a low carbon economy?' The answer was, of course, no. The report challenged industry to get to grips with the issue; the following recommendations get to the nub:

> *Recommendation 2.1: That as soon as a sufficiently rigorous assessment system is in place, the Treasury should introduce into the Green Book a requirement to conduct a whole-life (embodied + operational) carbon appraisal and that this is factored into feasibility studies on the basis of a realistic price for carbon.*
>
> *Recommendation 2.2: That the industry should agree with Government a standard method of measuring embodied carbon for use as a design tool and (as Recommendation 2.1) for the purposes of scheme appraisal.[3]*

In November 2011 the British Standard BS EN 15978:2011 was produced, essentially replicating CEN/TC 350 and bringing it into the British Standards framework. Unless repealed post-Brexit, this remains the point of reference. This standard sets out a whole life methodology, covering both operational carbon emissions and embodied emissions and including reuse, as per the circular economy. (See Chapter 6 for detail on BS EN 15978.) This represents the basis on which embodied and whole life carbon emissions are understood and assessed today. However, early use of BS EN 15978 led to incomparable assessments as different consultants, responding to clients with differing reporting requirements, interpreted the BS inconsistently.

In 2015, InnovateUK provided funding for a team (see Introduction for details) led by the author to produce an implementation plan for making BS EN 15978 consistent and understandable in use, and usable and accessible through RICS certification. The objective was to create a consistent plan for UK- and potentially EU-wide use that brings embodied and whole life carbon into the mainstream.

Carbon emissions in the built environment can be an odd concept to grasp, particularly with respect to materials. In the next sections, I explain what I understand by operational, embodied and whole life carbon emissions.

Operational carbon emissions

These are the emissions from energy used to operate a building. In the UK these are split into 'regulated' – namely those covered by legislation (Part L of the Building Regulations), such as heating, lighting and cooling – and 'unregulated', which covers small power use such as TVs, kettles, computers, fridges and so on. Reducing regulated emissions has a direct impact on the design of the building fabric through measures to reduce the need for energy consumption, such as increased insulation, double glazing, low energy lighting, etc. The Building Regulations (Part L) have evolved specifically to reduce the amount of energy used to heat, cool and light buildings, and have been very successful in improving the environmental performance of buildings.

The Passivhaus standard is an example of the optimum in environmental performance, in which regulated operational energy use is reduced to a practical minimum. This German-originated building standard provides for performance levels much higher than the UK Building Regulations, and is achieved through very high levels of insulation, airtightness, triple glazing, elimination of cold bridging and other measures.

The success of the UK Building Regulations has been in reducing building performance-related operational carbon emissions over the decades since their introduction. The point has been reached where further reductions, by way of further mitigation or the use of renewables, are becoming increasingly expensive – or, at least, are certainly perceived as being so (this is particularly true of many house builders, who see any increase in environmental standards as a direct cost). This view, although not necessarily accurate, particularly over the long term, has created a negative 'mood music' around sustainability and has led to the government backtracking on environmental legislation. For example, in October 2011 the then chancellor George Osborne, who prior to the 2010 election had promised that his Treasury would be 'a green ally, not a foe', told his party conference that saving the planet risked 'putting our country out of business'.[4]

Relative impacts of operational and embodied emissions

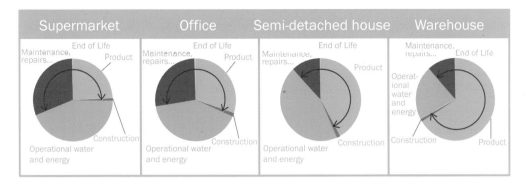

Figure 1.02: Relative impact of individual life cycle stages on the overall carbon footprint for different types of buildings, calculated over 30 years. Red arrows by author indicating embodied carbon proportion. (The energy results have been based on the Building Regulations.)

Analysis by the Royal Institute of Chartered Surveyors[5] and others shows that the proportion of embodied energy in relation to that of regulated operational energy is, in most new building typologies, greater than 50%, as shown in the above diagram where the green colour represents operational emissions. SCP has done similar analyses (see below) that support this view.

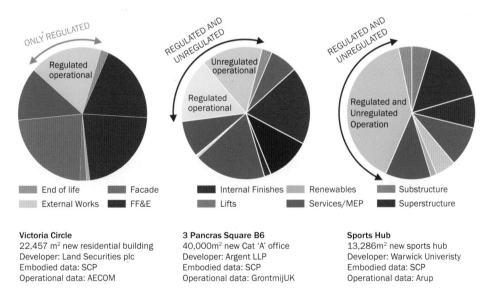

End of life	Facade	Internal Finishes	Renewables	Substructure	
External Works	FF&E	Lifts	Services/MEP	Superstructure	

Victoria Circle
22,457 m² new residential building
Developer: Land Securities plc
Embodied data: SCP
Operational data: AECOM

3 Pancras Square B6
40,000m² new Cat 'A' office
Developer: Argent LLP
Embodied data: SCP
Operational data: GrontmijUK

Sports Hub
13,286m² new sports hub
Developer: Warwick Univeristy
Embodied data: SCP
Operational data: Arup

Figure 1.03: WLC analyses – range differences between operational and embodied emissions.

Such data conflicts with a general perception that embodied carbon is a relatively small part of the overall lifetime emissions of most building types (see *What Colour is Your Building?* by David H. Clark, 2013, see Figure 3.07, page 51 – this section suggests that the embodied/operational ratio is 20%/80%).[6] This discrepancy can be partly attributed to the fact that, although buildings are becoming operationally more efficient all the time, the data reviews that have influenced thinking on the relative proportions tend to use data that predates the last few years, ie from before BREEAM 2011 and 2014 and Part L 2010 and 2013 effects were included. As buildings get more operationally efficient, so the embodied proportion increases.

The principal reasons however are that the following reporting deficiencies with reference to the BS EN 15978 modules have contributed to these discrepancies (see also Chapter 6):

1. **Under-reporting for modules A, B, and C:** This is generally down to reduced scope, since many assessments are only concerned with structure and cladding, ie they do not cover all elements of construction nor the interior fitout.

2. **Under-reporting for modules B2-B5:** Most assessments omit a proper analysis of maintenance, repair, replacement and refurbishment on the grounds of perceived complexity, or lack of knowledge. In practice, the life cycle emissions of these activities over 60 years can be significant: in the case of new office buildings, the embodied emissions over 60 years can be similar to those of the original construction. For example, for the Cat A office project T2, for Argent LLP, the approximate whole life carbon split at completion of RIBA Stage 3 was as follows.
    • Embodied carbon to practical completion: 36%
    • Embodied carbon over 60 years, plus disposal: 30%
    • Operational carbon (regulated and unregulated) over 60 years: 34%
    In the case of an owner-occupier, you would also have to include their internal upgrades over the 60-year period. This would significantly increase the embodied carbon proportions shown above.

3. **Under or non-reporting of module C:** Most assessments exclude a meaningful assessment of the end of life, ie the demolition and disposal carbon emissions. Although this can be difficult to analyse, it is an important consideration for resource-efficient design.

In aggregate, such under-reporting has meant that embodied carbon impacts have been misunderstood by the built environment industry. This is starting to change thanks to better understanding and better data, but it remains a significant point since it suggests that, while pressure to reduce operational emissions should continue, there are embodied (ie material-related) ways of making substantial carbon emissions reductions in the built environment at low or even zero cost. The implication is that, on the grounds of both cost and impact, the focus for carbon reductions in the built environment should spread to include embodied emissions in the form of a whole life approach. For architects and structural engineers, this means a shift in emphasis to materials and their efficient deployment rather than energy use efficiency, which is more in the remit of the services consultant.

Embodied carbon emissions (see Chapter 6 for methodology)

Sometimes also called embedded or capital carbon emissions, these are the emissions associated with the sourcing of raw material, transportation to a factory, fabrication into components and systems, delivery to site, and assembly into a building up to practical completion. Following completion, embodied emissions also refer to maintenance and replacement over an assumed building life expectancy, and final disassembly and disposal. Disposal can include reuse and recycling, meaning that redundant material is no longer waste but raw material for the next phase of use.

This holistic approach to reuse is referred to as the circular economy (see Chapter 3). Where conventional disposal such as landfill or incineration implies a high carbon cost, reuse and innovation can offer a lower carbon intensive outcome. Reduction measures can be introduced at all stages of the above sequence. The idea of the circular economy emphasises optimising the reuse of redundant products and materials, minimising the use of new material, and designing for future ease of reuse. All these aspects can be measured by their resulting carbon impacts. It is therefore possible through carbon accounting to compare the relative environmental performance of new v reuse. This concept is discussed in more detail in Chapter 3: case study 3.

The following sections refer to carbon reductions. What I mean by this is making material and life cycle choices to improve the carbon footprint of a component or system in relation to the baseline. In practice, when undertaking an assessment, we usually compare a building designed using industry standard measures to the same building using specifically selected measures. These might include use of recycled content, improved lifespan expectations, shorter transport distances, low carbon materials, more efficient construction, reduced waste, capacity for recycling, etc. This approach has limitations, so moving to a purely carbon emission cost per m^2 approach is recommended as it is simpler and allows for direct comparisons between buildings (as is already possible with build costs, rent, etc).

When examining a proposed building's potential for carbon reductions, there are many possible areas for consideration besides material selection. Transport distances can be reduced (local sourcing), waste can be reduced, and more efficient site management and construction planning can all make a difference. When considering the life of the building, designers need to consider ease of maintenance, omitting weak links from integrated systems to improve their lifespan, suitability (often durability) for purpose, ease of disassembly, avoidance of composite products, capacity for components and systems to be beneficially recycled, and the ultimate disposal of the building. The degree of flexibility within a building's overall design will also have embodied carbon impacts over time.

Embodied emissions are therefore a holistic assessment of the carbon emissions resulting from manipulating material from its original source via its use by society to its ultimate disposal. It follows that a key area of concern is the actual energy sources used in these processes. In the UK we rely predominantly on coal and gas, with nuclear increasing in proportion. France and Norway, for example, rely respectively on a greater proportion of nuclear and hydroelectric power than we do, resulting in lower carbon emissions from the use of the energy grid. Invariably, choosing a low carbon material solution involves analysing the various carbon costs such as source of fabrication energy v distance travelled, and so on.

Appropriate use of materials is an important feature of low carbon design. For example, which has the lower embodied carbon footprint – a brick wall or a timber fence? The answer lies in how long you want it, where it comes from, and how you dispose of the redundant material. If 100 years is your goal, then you may need many timber fences, as opposed to one wall. Alternatively if you want a temporary structure, the brick option would be a waste of resources.

It is worth making a comment on timber sequestration at this point. Timber is generally seen as a 'green' material. As the above example shows, this is not necessarily the case. One way to think of this is whether your use of timber is better or worse than the natural cycle. Trees capture carbon dioxide over a natural lifespan before they die and rot away. If you accelerate this process, then you are speeding up the CO_2e release process. If you are slowing it down, by 'locking' timber into the building and ultimately disposing of it in a way that is better than allowing it to rot, then you are improving on the natural cycle. Also important with timber is waste minimisation and disposal, and using glues that don't have poor greenhouse gas consequences.

Whole life carbon (see Chapter 6 for methodology)

The simple definition of whole life carbon is the total sum of the operational and embodied emissions expended over a building's whole life. However, implicit in the concept of 'whole life' is that by considering operational and embodied emissions together you optimise the relationship and ensure the lowest overall emissions reduction.

Today the idea of carbon emissions reduction is generally understood as reducing operational, ie day-to-day, energy usage. As previously noted, this is not surprising for historical reasons, and the Building Regulations, BREEAM and Town Planning requirements all encourage taking action to reduce such usage either through enhancing the performance of the building fabric, or by introducing renewable energy sources. In isolation such actions do of course reduce operational energy use. However, crucially, the embodied carbon cost of such actions is not taken into account. This is like counting the rent received from a property without factoring in the cost of building it; for example, making, delivering and installing insulation has a carbon cost.

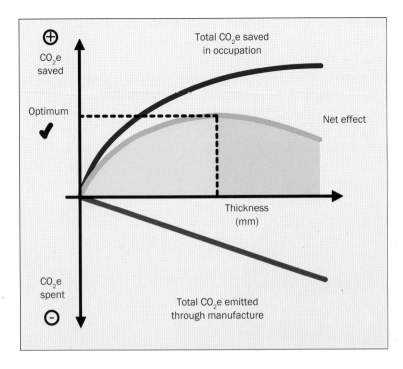

Total CO₂e saved in occupation — $Total\ CO_2e\ saved\ in\ occupation$

(Figure labels, reading as on chart:)

⊕
CO_2e saved

Total CO_2e saved
in occupation

Optimum
✔

Net effect

Thickness
(mm)

CO_2e
spent

⊖

Total CO_2e emitted
through manufacture

Figure 1.04: Carbon emissions reduction and resource efficiency – insulation example. Past an optimum point additional insulation is more damaging than beneficial.

Figure 1.04 above shows that increasing the thickness of insulation increases the operational benefit (blue line), but at a diminishing rate, and with a linear carbon cost (red line). The net effect cost/benefit line (in green) shows that past a certain point additional insulation is actually more destructive than beneficial in carbon emissions terms. This 'capcarb' versus 'opcarb' combination is crucial in understanding the true carbon cost of assembling and using buildings. It also means that materials energy usage, and not only operational usage, should be considered over time. For a proper assessment of a building's carbon performance, it is necessary to first understand the interrelationship between material and operational carbon emissions and, second, the performance of both over time. BS EN 15978 covers this in overall terms and describes the various stages from sourcing of materials through usage, maintenance, refurbishment and final disposal.

This whole life approach to carbon emissions has profound implications for the way we design buildings. Focusing solely on operational energy expenditure has historically been both sensible and necessary and has meant that new buildings are operationally efficient to the extent that regulated operational emissions often account for less than half the total lifetime (frequently 60 years) emissions of a building (see page 14). This is thanks, in varying degrees, to Part L, BREEAM, the now defunct Code for Sustainable Homes, EPCs and DECs.

Therefore, as most of the easy wins, including renewables, are increasingly incorporated into current building design, further cost-effective emissions reductions can only be achieved through more efficient and targeted use of material resources. These embodied emissions savings entail us thinking much more carefully about the sourcing and delivery of materials used, the opportunities for using recycled materials, the methods of fabrication, the quantity of waste produced in assembling components and buildings and, most importantly, what happens over the life of a building. Designers have to think about what happens to their buildings after they have been completed, what the desired life expectancy is, how the building is maintained, and how it will be dismantled and disposed of. The carbon cost of a building over its life is linked directly to these issues. The 'recyclability' of a building is key to considering its overall footprint.

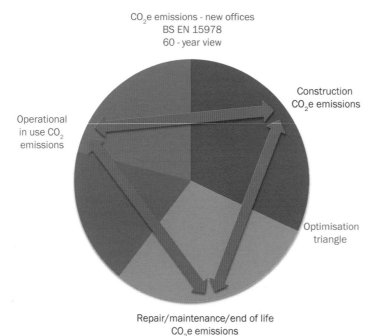

CO_2e emissions - new offices
BS EN 15978
60 - year view

Construction
CO_2e emissions

Operational
in use CO_2
emissions

Optimisation
triangle

Repair/maintenance/end of life
CO_2e emissions

Figure 1.05: Whole life costs – typical carbon emissions of new offices over 60 years (according to BS EN 15978). This diagram is an average of several new-build office projects in central London.

Figure 1.05 above shows the 'optimisation triangle', ie the three areas of emissions that make up a building's whole life performance. The proportions shown are averaged and relate to several typical, new, high-specification 'shell and core' speculative office buildings. The key to a genuinely low carbon building is to understand and optimise the relationships between these three areas; what makes this difficult is the reliability of the information available for each area. The proportions shown are based on design stage assessments. However, it is clear from post-occupancy evaluation that the regulated operational design stage assessments can be incorrect by a factor of 1.5 to 2.5 or even more when compared to actual usage (see www.CarbonBuzz. org).[7] It is disturbing that building design, and certain planning requirements (eg offsets against Part L), are therefore frequently based on incorrectly projected operational energy usage. That being said, the system works to the extent that the operational performance of buildings is being continually improved, even if actual use patterns are not known.

It should, in theory, be possible to be as precise about the embodied emissions cost of construction as we are about cost estimates at the design stage assessments. By practical completion, it is certainly possible to know with a high degree of accuracy the embodied emissions cost (ie what went into making the building and where it all came from). It is more difficult to accurately assess the embodied life cycle carbon emissions costs as there are a great many variables, we don't know what the future life of the building will be, and there is not enough accumulated data. However, it is likely that embodied life cycle assessments for a continuously occupied building could have a similar margin of error to operational emissions assessments. Ultimately, as with operational emissions analysis, the very fact of assessing the future embodied carbon life cycle makes us think about what happens to materials and systems post practical completion – even if this involves making assumptions about the future. This provides useful design stage information to guide us towards designing better buildings with lower whole life carbon footprints.

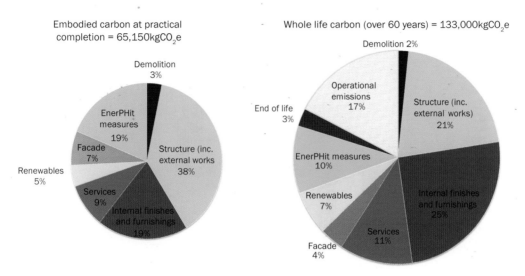

Figure 1.06: Carbon emissions of an EnerPHit residential retrofit project for Grosvenor – on the left at practical completion, and on the right over 60 years. Note the proportion of operational emissions. The diagram on the left will be more accurate than that on the right. The right-hand diagram makes assumptions with respect to the replacement of services, interiors, roof coverings, PVs, triple-glazed units and maintenance.

Thinking past practical completion will improve the overall performance of buildings, reduce carbon emissions and reduce lifetime financial costs by ensuring buildings are easier to maintain and dismantle. It will also change the architectural expression of buildings as the implication of low carbon choices and life cycle thinking take root. Also implicit in whole life thinking, and thinking about a building's performance post practical completion, is factoring in the impacts of future climate change. By giving consideration to potential temperature increases of some 1.5-4°C by 2100,[8] we encourage more resource-efficient buildings, reduce future overheating, and design in future adaptability.

Low carbon thinking is, in essence, the efficient use of resources, and as such also aligns directly with low initial construction costs. Sustainability has the image of being an extra cost to a project. In fact, sustainability is about long-term value. In general, low carbon thinking and better material choices should not add to the cost of a project in the long term. There are many examples where a whole life carbon analysis produces a cheaper outcome.

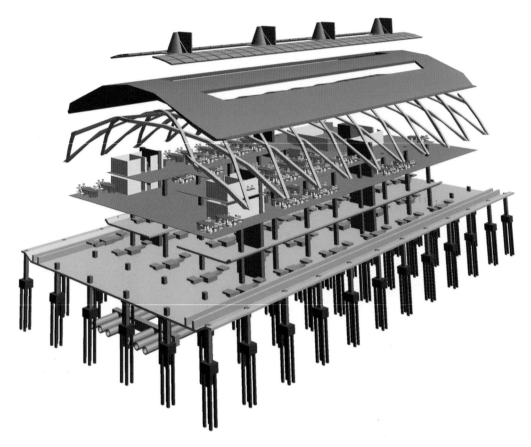

Figure 1.07: System analysis for World Wildlife Fund – Living Planet Centre. This is done to understand the relationship of the lifespans of different elements.

This project for the World Wildlife Fund shows the outcome of comparing the embodied and operational carbon costs of double and triple glazing. Assessed over a 60-year period, the lower carbon whole life option was double glazing. This was because the carbon cost of the third sheet of glass, including the additional framing, and allowing for replacement at around 40 years, was greater than the additional heating-related emissions over the same period. In addition, the capital cost difference was lower for double glazing, with only a marginal increase in running costs. This example shows the necessity of taking a whole life view when assessing the carbon impacts of a design decision. In this case, focusing solely on operational emissions would have produced the higher carbon cost and the higher financial cost. The operational performance data was by Atelier 10; the embodied performance data was by SCP.

Whole life carbon – practical application

Reducing embodied and whole life carbon through the RIBA work stages

It is possible at every RIBA stage to examine options to reduce the whole life carbon cost of a building.[1] To optimise the overall carbon reduction potential of a project, each stage should be considered from the outset. Every building should be thought of as an organism that evolves over time after it is 'finished'; the architects and engineers who design it are responsible for setting up the most carbon-efficient process for the building's whole life. The following is a summary of how a 'carbon consultant' (CC) might work within a project team. Chapter 6 sets out the calculation methodology for each of the BS EN 15978 modules. This methodology would be used in the context of RIBA project stages as explained below.

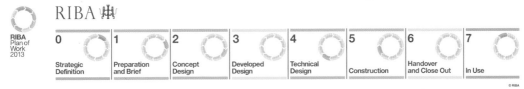

Figure 2.01: RIBA Plan of Work 2013 – stages.

RIBA STAGE 0 – strategic definition

The starting point is a client decision to include embodied and whole life carbon (WLC) accounting within project objectives as a key performance indicator – a choice that clients are increasingly making. The principal reasons for undertaking WLC assessments include: producing a specifically low carbon building, futureproofing asset value by pre-empting changes in standards and legislation, marketing advantages, corporate social responsibility, circular economic considerations, added value, resource efficiency, or a genuine desire to reduce the impact on climate change.

RIBA STAGE 1 – preparation and brief

WLC would typically be seen as part of 'sustainability aspirations' within the project objectives. It would therefore be necessary to define for the project team what must be achieved through WLC assessment. Implicit in WLC is life cycle assessment (LCA). This encourages the design team to engage with long-term thinking about the building's fabric and functional performance past practical completion. A carbon consultant must be selected to provide the required level of advice.

This should ideally cover all modules (ie A, B, C, D) of BS EN 15978 (for more detail see Chapter 6), and all RIBA stages.

RIBA STAGE 2 – concept design

WLC thinking should be embedded within the design process from the outset. Even at a conceptual stage, the issues of materiality and life cycle thinking play their part. LCA considerations such as climate change, future building flexibility, intended life and durability, materiality, deconstruction and disposal are all relevant to concept development. The carbon consultant can assist with concept development by providing comparative WLC assessments of various building fabric options being considered, as well as the carbon cost/benefit relationship with operational environmental strategies. WLC analysis can contribute to BREEAM 2014, specifically: Mat 01 Life cycle impacts; Mat 04 Insulation; Man 02 Life Cycle Costing; Ene 01 Reduction of energy use and carbon emissions; Wst 01 Construction waste management; Wst 02 Recycled aggregates.

Generally, design teams have little or no experience of embodied and whole life carbon reduction. It is therefore important for the carbon consultant to start with a team workshop to explain the process, issues and what is required. This form of introductory communication is key to success.

RIBA STAGE 3 – developed design

WLC analyses of the more detailed options under consideration – typically structural and envelope options – and the relationship with the building's proposed environmental performance should be undertaken. The carbon consultant should be working closely with the project team. A 'carbon budget' should be prepared using the stage 2 or stage 3 cost plan's material descriptions and quantities. This will form the baseline carbon budget against which improvements can be judged. A life cycle analysis will be undertaken to enable an assessment of the carbon life cycle costs over the building's desired lifespan. This LCA should be synchronised with any life cycle costing (as part of Man 02, usually by the QS). The carbon budget can be presented as a total carbon cost and/ or as a m² rate. Typically a list of detailed options and their impact on the carbon budget would be prepared to enable the design team to choose low carbon, and preferably cost neutral, options.

WLC can contribute to planning applications, although even the most enthusiastic local authorities are usually not yet familiar with, nor yet have policies to accept, embodied carbon savings in lieu of shortfalls against Part L. SCP has had some success in using embodied savings to offset operational shortfalls.

The last part of this chapter contains two case studies, on structure and cladding. These are examples of the detailed thinking that can contribute to better design choices.

RIBA stage 4 – technical design

Low carbon choices made during stage 3 are now integrated into the detailed drawings, specifications and tender documentation, with further support from local assessments. The carbon budget should be updated and included within the tender documentation. It is important that the tender documentation ensures that the tendering contractors understand the WLC requirements, the goals, and the process of delivering and monitoring carbon reductions during construction. This process needs to be tailored to engage with but not burden the supply chain.

Low carbon strategies developed at the design stage will come to nothing unless they can be delivered during procurement. With any tendering process there are a number of actions that can facilitate this. Whatever the procurement route, and particularly with design and build, it is vital that the tender documentation includes clear and understandable WLC information. It is also important to ensure that the way carbon-related information is asked for during tender does not increase project costs. Generally, if tendering contractors are engaged in the process from the outset, it is not difficult for them to buy into a low carbon process. In fact, many contractors are enthusiastic and contribute to what is essentially a resource efficiency exercise that is as beneficial to them as it is to the client or the planet. Education and early explanation of requirements is crucial, as for many main contractors, and certainly for those in the supply chain (tier one and tier two subcontractors), this is new territory.

RIBA stage 5 – construction

The key issue is monitoring the actual carbon impacts of the construction process against the carbon budget, and what has been agreed on completion of the tender process. To ensure continuing focus, and depending on project size and scope, reporting at intervals of every three to six months ensures that problems or proposed design changes can be managed from a carbon perspective. In this sense, monitoring the carbon budget is not dissimilar to monitoring the construction costs. Proposed WLC and life cycle impacts of variations can be brought to the client's attention.

Efficiency and carbon emissions reduction go hand in hand. Efficient construction entails efficient use of resources, which reduces both costs and carbon emissions. Monitoring the delivery of commitments made during design and procurement is essential to ensure delivery of a low carbon building. The pressures of programme and cost can conspire to water down these commitments. Client support is crucial, and with design and build in particular it is necessary to create contractual mechanisms to ensure enforcement of targets. Typically, with good early engagement, most contractors see these issues as beneficial to them as well as the client.

Post practical completion, the carbon consultant should undertake a final review of the 'as built' information and produce a final assessment of the WLC impacts of the completed project.

The final version of the LCA should be included within the O&M manual. The final assessment should be compared to the initial budgets so that lessons can be learned.

> As with any process requiring positive action, verification and assessment of the completed product is vital. Knowledge of the post-completion assessment requirement helps ensure compliance. The completion assessment can include certification that a certain embodied carbon footprint has been achieved.

RIBA Stage 7 – in use

Any post-occupancy evaluation (PoE) should take account of the WLC impacts. This should include the fabrics' physical performance, and an assessment of maintenance regimes.

> Buildings are living things in the sense that they change and deteriorate in response to environmental impacts and the actions of the occupants. How a building evolves over its life is very much down to decisions made at the design stages. The carbon intensity of maintenance, repair and refurbishment can be substantially affected by both the initial design solutions, and the regimes in place to manage the building. The latter is similar to environmental control systems, which, if poorly managed, can substantially increase running costs.

Low carbon design choices

Design choices made at each RIBA stage will affect the carbon cost of the final building. The following gives some idea of the considerations that help to achieve low WLC outcomes. Low carbon design is a state of mind that should ideally become second nature, to the same extent as designing for gravity, rain and sunlight.

Existing resources

Establish which materials, structure and fabric already on site are suitable for reuse within the project. Retention of structure and major components are significant benefits as they remove demolition, transportation of waste, disposal, new fabrication, more transportation and construction of new components from the carbon cost equation. Recycling of existing material within the scheme is the next best thing, provided that it results in lower overall emissions compared to new. Recycling that involves carbon-intensive transport away from site, energy-intensive reworking, and transport back to site, will probably not contribute to a lower footprint, even if the recycled content proportion looks high. Existing resources for which there is no further use should be disposed of as efficiently as possible, preferably for beneficial recycling (for which there are an increasing number of material-specific recycling companies, and websites such as Recipro-UK.com).

Part of the conceptual approach is to consider what the next architect/engineer would do with your building when it comes to future refurbishment. Can your building be dismantled and recycled in its entirety? Can the components be reused at the same level, ie not just at a lower use level? The ideal is for nothing to be wasted, and everything to be reusable.

Designing for flexibility from the outset makes it easier for a building to be reused in its entirety in a different use class. This also presupposes a high level of durability in the external fabric, as well as architectural design quality. Well-designed buildings have social and economic benefits for both the occupier and the locality. People enjoy good architecture and that contributes to its retention, whereas poor architecture is often rejected by society, leading to early demolition (a very poor carbon outcome).

In conclusion, resource-efficient low carbon design should start with what is available on site for reuse. This is not often done; our cultural demand for the new produces vast amounts of unnecessary waste.

Environmental strategy

The relationship between operational and embodied emissions and their collective mitigation is key to a low carbon building. Mechanical systems not only use energy but require maintenance and replacement on a relatively short life cycle. Fabricating, transporting and disposing of such systems is energy- and carbon-intensive. Passive systems are therefore sensible for both operational and embodied emission reduction.

The performance of services and the relative merits of different environmental systems are not the subject of this book. However, the carbon cost of installing and maintaining services is an important feature of a building's lifetime carbon cost. Mechanical systems are energy-intensive to make, and do not have a long life expectancy. Central plant is usually replaced after 20-25 years, as are lift systems. Most sophisticated heating, cooling and renewable energy systems have comparatively short life expectancies (15-25 years). In addition, the materials that go into fabricating mechanical systems are often high quality and high on embodied energy fabrication costs. This combination of high initial carbon cost and short life expectancy, in addition to the operational running costs, means that mechanically managed environments are very poor carbon performers on all fronts. Efficiently designed building fabric and 'natural' strategies reduce or even omit the need for mechanical systems.

The corollary is that buildings that manage their environments without the use of mechanical systems have lower overall whole life carbon footprints. Omitting mechanical systems omits a large part of a building's regulated operational energy use, and the embodied costs of the plant. However, the equation is incomplete without factoring in the carbon costs of naturally ventilated or renewable energy systems. The Everyman Theatre in Liverpool (2014 Stirling Prize winner) has large brick towers to provide a natural ventilation strategy. These have a carbon cost (mitigated by using recycled brick already on site) but also a very long life expectancy. Both the lifetime carbon and financial costs will therefore be low.

Figure 2.02: Everyman Theatre, Liverpool.

A whole life carbon analysis of a project will examine the carbon cost, including any support infrastructure, of the proposed renewables in relation to the carbon benefits over the life expectancy of the project. It is a simple matter of comparing costs and benefits from the carbon emissions perspective. Typically cost/benefit analysis with respect to renewables is purely financial, and omits the carbon cost/benefit, which can be misleading.

Primary structure

The structural systems for buildings are many and varied. All systems have a carbon cost to source and assemble. However, the key to a low carbon structural strategy is to select the optimal system not just for the immediate requirement, and for the desired life expectancy, but also for future flexibility. This means optimising use of recycled content and considering the ultimate potential for reuse, either whole or in components. Many architects, such as Waugh Thistleton, Hopkins, PLP and SOM, are challenging preconceptions as to what this means and are exploring ways of using timber as primary structure in large buildings.

Some solutions such as steel or timber can be designed for easy dismantling and reuse. Concrete, using cement replacements, recycled content in steel, and recycled aggregate can be relatively carbon-efficient, particularly if durability and long life are required. Post-tensioned slabs use less concrete than a regular flat slab or reinforced concrete slab and deck combination, but are also less flexible for future adaptation such as creating new voids or moving shear walls. Typically, these structural choices are determined by the cost and procurement options around the initial construction, and not by longer-term, post-completion considerations. Owner-occupiers are best placed to take a long-term view; however, the design and construction industry does not generally provide life cycle choices to such clients, nor act to ensure that such buildings are designed for an efficient or evolving life past practical completion.

Structure-related emissions reduction strategies are important for achieving low carbon buildings since that is where, proportionately, most of the carbon reductions can be found.

Case study 1 is a comparative analysis of several structural systems from the carbon footprint perspective. It shows the issues that should be considered when determining the carbon cost of structural options.

External walls and cladding

The design of the external skin has a variety of performance demands: environmental, cost and aesthetic. It is directly linked to the environmental management of the internal spaces, and whether the building is passively or mechanically ventilated. There are several principal parameters that need to be considered in relation to optimising the overall (embodied and operational) performance of a facade. These are the initial embodied carbon costs of construction, the lifetime embodied carbon costs through maintenance and disposal, the potential for deconstruction and reuse, and the lifetime operational performance costs consequent on the design. The relationship between these parameters depends on required life expectancy and desired lifetime performance. Inappropriate choices can have significant unnecessary carbon costs.

The Library of Birmingham, a 2014 RIBA Stirling Prize finalist, uses what is essentially an office cladding system with circular aluminium decorative elements. This type of system typically has a life expectancy of no more than about 40 years. The owners will also have to deal with the significant financial and carbon costs of replacing the cladding after this short timeframe. The redundant materials will have to be disposed of (preferably recycled), and the owners will have to consider how to re-clad the building under what is likely to be a much more stringent regulatory regime. A more robust facade might have had a higher initial carbon cost but, if it lasts longer and is capable of incremental repair (ie replacing windows in a 'hole in wall' typology), then it may be the most carbon-efficient solution in the long term. The Birmingham example is, sadly, representative of the short-term thinking typical of much contemporary architecture.

Figure 2.03: The Library of Birmingham – a public building using a comparatively short-life, office-type, powder-coated aluminium cladding system.

Another 2014 Stirling Prize finalist is the Shard in London, which has a unitised double skin (single- plus double-glazed) cladding system designed to provide operational performance benefits. However, the Shard houses a variety of uses (offices, residential, hotel, retail), all of which have different lease lengths. What will happen to the occupants when the cladding has to be replaced in 40-plus years' time? This will entail a carbon and financial cost at a time when, in accordance with the low carbon transition plan, the UK should be achieving 80% CO_2 reductions against 1990 levels. The facade's unitised system gives the Shard a further disadvantage. Unitised systems typically interlock across an entire building, making it difficult – if not impossible – to replace part of the cladding in line with lease expiries.

It is interesting to compare the Shard with One Canada Square, the Canary Wharf tower, which was completed in 1990. This has stainless steel cladding but with a 'hole in wall' elevation so that the high-performance windows can be individually removed and replaced. This means that incremental upgrading, ie floor by floor, can happen in sync with lease cycles or even deterioration of sections of the facade. The stainless steel cladding has a comparatively high carbon cost of production, but this is mitigated by its very long life expectancy. Overall, One Canada Square's cladding strategy seems more carbon-efficient, flexible and financially efficient in the long term than the Shard's.

Figure 2.04: The Shard (2014). High carbon investment, limited lifespan (approximately 40-50 years) cladding. The unitised system makes incremental replacement very difficult.

Figure 2.05: One Canada Square (1990). This building has been designed with 'hole in wall' type cladding. Individual windows or floors can have windows replaced to suit lease cycles.

The idea that it is acceptable for major new buildings to have a short life expectancy is a relatively recent one. The construction of a new building takes a significant amount of material and energy resources, so the life expectancy of the finished item and how it is disposed of have great importance from a carbon emissions perspective. When it comes to buildings with very short life requirements, the maintenance aspects are less important; the focus should be on low carbon materials for the initial construction, the potential for dismantling and reuse for the whole building, and/or recycling of components and systems. What happens to the building when it is no longer required should be an integral part of the initial design philosophy.

An interesting example of short-term building is the Serpentine Pavilion, the annual temporary art gallery in London's Kensington Gardens. This is always a signature building showcasing the latest in design thinking; in 2016 it was designed by the Danish firm BIG. The pavilion represents a carbon investment in a building that is required only for a short period. What it is made of, what the construction emissions are and what happens to it once it is no longer required are all relevant questions in a post-COP 21 world.

What is instructive about the Serpentine commission, and BIG's design as an example, is that it represents the opposite problem to the one we normally face, ie ensuring durability and long-term thinking when it comes to an efficient use of resources. Instead the issue is the appropriate carbon cost of a building that is only required for a few months. The nature of the architecture itself may provide the solution. If the building is considered as an organism, rather than a static object, then its time as a pavilion may only be a short part of a much longer, more varied and maybe even dispersed life. The nature of the assembly allows it to morph into many different things.

BIG's pavilion is made from glass fibre-reinforced plastic (GRP), a lightweight, oil-based material, with these particular units being made in Denmark. Denmark has a very sustainable electricity grid (less than 50% the carbon density of the UK's) and the embodied carbon of the manufacturing process is therefore very low. If the carbon cost of the pavilion were spread over its three-month life and then incinerated on demolition, this would be a bad carbon outcome. However, after completing its term at the Serpentine, the pavilion was then reinstalled across Asia and the US. Its prefabricated nature means it can be disassembled and reassembled with minimal effort; transport is the principal carbon cost. After that, it is a question of whether the components can be reassembled into another use entirely.

What happens at the end of life is still a concern with GRP. It can be used as a fuel source, or alternatively as a form of recycled aggregate. Of course, there are other materials with a lower inherent carbon cost and less damaging disposal costs that could have produced a better overall whole life carbon cost.

So, this particular pavilion does have reuse benefits that mitigate its overall carbon impact. The use of oil-based products is not great but is mitigated by the efficiency of Denmark's power grid. I would challenge future Serpentine Pavilions to be designed with full resource efficiency to make the minimum carbon impact and be 100% recyclable. It could be a truly zero carbon building and an exemplar of circular economic thinking. This is surely the environmentally and socially responsible thing to do.

Figure 2.06: Serpentine Gallery Pavilion by BIG. Short life, but capable of relocation and reassembly.

Interiors

The interior design and fitout of buildings change on a much shorter life cycle than the structure and shell. Therefore, while the initial carbon cost of fitout may be comparatively small in relation to structure or cladding, the aggregate carbon cost can exceed these large initial capital carbon cost items over the life of a building, particularly in commercial or public buildings that have heavy use or churn (see Figure 6.06 on Page 115 Chapter 6). From the outset, interiors decisions need to be strategic from a future maintenance perspective as much as aesthetic and cost driven. Natural finishes such as brick, which do not need a finishing layer or regular maintenance, fit a low carbon strategy on both counts.

Retail is an area that generally has a comparatively high interior design turnover with consequently high carbon costs. But there are exceptions – Apple stores are simple and sparse with a resulting low carbon life cycle cost. Retailers such as Marks & Spencer are making significant efforts to understand and mitigate the issue by, for example, careful material selection and omitting ceilings in their Simply Food stores.

The issue of recyclability is crucial where high interior turnover is necessary. The more redundant material can be beneficially recycled, the lower the overall carbon cost. A well-known technology company, for example, has a dynamic and creative approach to its interior spatial requirements that entails a short life cycle for some interior components but also flexible layouts. Lifetime carbon costs are kept to a minimum by a combination of low carbon initial choices, including recycled content, high reuse potential, and partitioning systems that are easily demountable and reusable.

Office interiors are often problematic, typically with high carbon cost entrance halls, and entire ceiling systems being disposed of when not required by the incoming occupier. However, developers are increasingly avoiding fitting out office space until a tenant is secured and their requirements known. This avoids significant carbon and financial waste.

See Chapter 6 for more information on the relationship between carbon, money and life cycle.

CASE STUDY 1:

Whole life carbon – structural systems

BY ATHINA PAPAKOSTA

This case study was originally complied for an article in *Building* magazine.[2] The aim was to compare the carbon emissions associated with choosing different structural systems. It has been edited and adapted for inclusion here.

The selection of a structural system is key to non-domestic developments from an architectural, stability and cost perspective, but it is also highly influential on the embodied carbon side. The structure constitutes the backbone of the building and is the longest serving set of elements. Given the above, getting it right in all aspects is essential. The focus of this study is the impact of different structural systems on whole life carbon. A range of typical structural forms featuring the three main structural constituent materials – concrete, steel and timber – have been comparatively examined in terms of embodied carbon and cost. Beyond that, the substantial role of careful design and material specification in the overall carbon emissions, as well as end of life (EoL) scenarios and the concepts of futureproofing, designing for reuse, and the recyclability of structural components have been explored.

Material elements of structural systems

The three main materials used for structural purposes are concrete, steel and timber. Simple, low-rise housing schemes often feature load-bearing brick and block masonry but these are deemed outside of the scope of this study. The aforementioned have been established as the predominant constituents of structural elements due to their robustness, particular characteristics and initial relative abundance. However, growing construction activity results in material scarcity, making resource efficiency increasingly important. Combating climate change is also encouraging mitigation of carbon emissions.

Concrete

Figure 2.07: Concrete-framed structure in London

The concrete industry accounts for approximately 5% of the total manmade CO_2 emissions. Concrete has good compression and stiffness properties and high density. The main ingredients of concrete mixes are cement, aggregate and water. Cement is the most carbon-intensive item due to the mining process, but it can be substituted to a degree with by-products from other industries (eg GGBS, originating from steel manufacture, or PFA, originating from coal burning). Cement replacement results in substantial carbon reductions without compromising the structural performance. The substitute materials are also marginally cheaper than Portland cement. Over 40-50% cement replacement with GGBS may have implications for the construction programme due to longer concrete curing times. However, if the specification calls for more than 50% GGBS replacement, any potential delays can be accommodated with early consideration and careful scheduling.

As far as aggregate is concerned, the use of secondary/recycled aggregates is encouraged where it does not compromise structural performance, ie not requiring higher cement rates to achieve the same strength. Travel distances also need to be considered.

Steel reinforcement provides the necessary tensile strength but contributes additional carbon cost to concrete structures. However, it is by now standard practice for steel reinforcement rods produced in Europe to be fabricated using secondary steel scrap, ie recycled material.

Timber formwork is the most common form of shuttering; however, it is often used no more than a handful of times as it can get damaged in the pouring process. It is crucial that poor material management is avoided and timber waste does not get landfilled but reused or incinerated, as when left to rot it emits CO_2 as well as methane (CH_4, with a global warming potential about 25 times higher than CO_2). Steel or plastic reusable formwork systems are recommended from a carbon emissions perspective as they can be used multiple times.

Concrete has operational benefits due to its thermal mass in that it can act as a heat store to alleviate heating and cooling loads. This needs to be factored in with the operational emissions of a building to understand the whole life carbon picture.

Steel

Structural steel provides great strength with a relatively low weight. It is therefore widely used in construction and in numerous other fields and contributes about 5% of the total anthropogenic carbon emissions attributed to the steel industry. Steel is 100% recyclable without degrading in quality over its life, enabling recycling and reuse multiple times, which means that secondary steel (scrap steel) has an economic value, leading to recovery rates of over 90%.

Steel from virgin iron ore – primary production – is manufactured in basic oxygen furnaces (BOF) with a small percentage of scrap, while secondary steel, mainly from scrap, is fabricated in electric arc furnaces (EAF). The EAF process is less carbon-intensive than BOF both in terms of raw materials as well as manufacturing-related emissions.

Structural steel used in construction also requires fire protection, which must be factored into any carbon performance comparison.

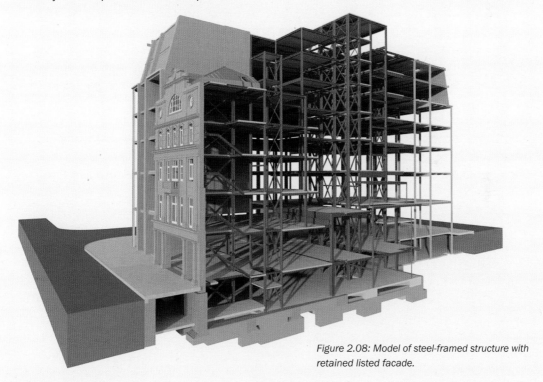

Figure 2.08: Model of steel-framed structure with retained listed facade.

Timber

A basic starting point is that any timber used should be sustainably sourced, holding an FSC or equivalent certification. Trees absorb CO_2 through photosynthesis during their growth. After being cut down and fabricated, the benefit of the carbon they have captured and stored can be claimed – the so-called carbon sequestration.

In general, for simple structural timber more CO_2 is captured during growth than emitted through fabrication. Disposal is key and landfilling should be avoided as noted in the point above about timber shuttering. Another area to consider is the specific preservatives and adhesives used in fabricating composite timber elements, such as glued laminated timber (GLULAM) and cross-laminated timber (CLT), which can release harmful substances including CO_2.

Structural systems

The most popular structural solutions across the UK commercial building stock, including residential blocks, were selected to be analysed for this study: reinforced concrete (RC) frame, post-tensioned concrete (PT RC) frame, steel frame with metal decking, and steel frame with CLT slabs (the latter being less commonly used). The relative contribution of superstructure to the total embodied carbon of different commercial building projects SCP has worked on is substantial: 44% on average, ranging between 30 and 64%, depending on the circumstances.

The durability of all structural systems investigated has been assumed to be equivalent and to exceed 60 years. The case study buildings used were office type. Several variants have been modelled for each of the main structure types to account for different design specifications, and the embodied carbon has been calculated for each. The focus has been on the various types of superstructure, while the substructure – piled foundations – has been assumed to be the same across all options and proportionate to the dead weight of the superstructure. The live loads remain unchanged for all case studies as they are all the same building type. Images and additional guidance have been kindly provided by HTS structural engineers.

The bar graph in figure 2.09 illustrates the whole life carbon footprint of each of the variants per m² of Gross internal (floor) area (GIA) of the building. The embodied carbon of the substructure is hatched with oblique lines while the embodied carbon of superstructures is shown in solid bars, each colour representing the overarching structural system type. The pale grey bars display carbon emissions related to the structures' EoL. Regarding the systems featuring timber, the orange shaded rectangles with the arrow pointing down represent the carbon sequestered.

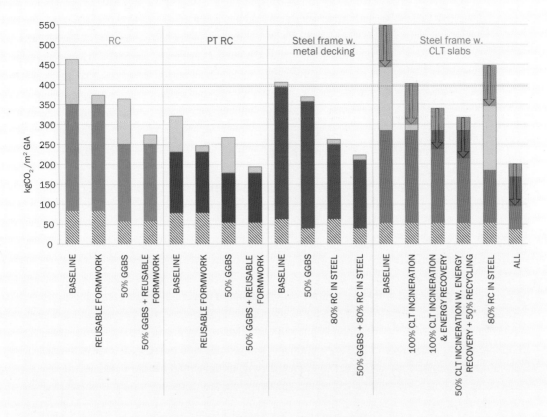

Figure 2.09: Comparative graph of the carbon emissions per m² GIA of the different variations of the structural systems analysed.

COST SUMMARY	RC	PT RC	Steel frame w. ribdeck	Steel frame w. CLT
Superstructure	210-285 £/m² GIA	280-380 £/m² GIA	255-345 £/m² GIA	300-410 £/m² GIA
Total	265-355 £/m² GIA	350-475 £/m² GIA	325-445 £/m² GIA	380-515 £/m² GIA

Table 2.01: Average cost range for different structural systems in the UK.
Source: SCP Data (Athina Papakosta)

As demonstrated in figure 2.09, the EoL carbon emissions due to any sort of organic waste – either formwork for the RC and PT RC structures or CLT floor slabs – contribute a substantial share to the whole life picture. The variation in the results reveals sizeable carbon reduction potential for all types of structures against the respective baselines for basic specification. The standard RC frame has been considered as the baseline. The total whole life carbon of the different options varied between up to +18% for conventional steel frame with CLT slabs if the timber gets landfilled, and up to -58% for concrete frame with PT slabs using 50% GGBS cement replacement against the RC baseline, as shown in table 2.01.

The steel frame options are fairly high in embodied carbon due to the base assumption of 20% recycled content in steel, which results in about 1.7 times higher embodied carbon compared to the more commonly used average of 60% recycled content for steel products. 20% recycled content was selected as it represents the current UK market average for steel sections more accurately; 60% is an average across all steel products and not specifically structural steel profiles. Based on the same logic, 100% recycled content has been set as the baseline for steel bar reinforcement.

Looking at the steel frame with CLT slabs variant, it is apparent that the EoL carbon impact of timber is decisive and should be considered from the outset. Timber can be a highly sustainable material option if care is taken to avoid the considerable carbon footprint arising from its decomposition or incineration where the produced heat is not put to use.

Designing for the future – end of life, circular economy, reuse, recycling

The EoL figures presented in this case study clearly highlight the importance of considering a whole life perspective for structural systems, as opposed to the common perception that such elements have no further carbon implications beyond practical completion as they do not require any maintenance or replacement over the life cycle of a building. To create more environmentally conscious buildings, the reusability, recyclability and further potential EoL scenarios of structural elements must be incorporated into the decision-making process from an early design stage.

The adaptability of structures is also key as it determines a building's capacity to cater for future needs. A flexible structural design is more likely to be retained in the future as it will respond well to change and so contribute to a lower overall carbon footprint. 'Flexibility' in this context can mean the ability to accommodate different uses. It can also mean demountable structural elements, eg precast concrete floor planks of standardised spans, or bolted instead of welded steel connections. These are useful ways to ensure adaptability and reusability within the context of resource efficiency and the circular economy. Fitness for purpose in a holistic sense, balancing durability and flexibility, should be a key driver for optimising the design.

Conclusions

The type of structural system chosen is highly influential on a building's layout as well as on the type and quantities of materials to be used. It also has a big impact on embodied and whole life carbon. End of life needs to be considered from the outset to enable future adaptations and minimise carbon cost. Any of the structural systems examined can result in low carbon solutions if they are efficiently designed and carefully specified in terms of materials and EoL treatment. Reusing and recycling of elements is an effective carbon reduction and resource efficiency measure and constitutes the basis of circular economy.

CASE STUDY 2:

Whole life carbon – curtain walling

BY LEO CHEUNG AND MIRKO FARNETANI

This case study is based on SCP's work on a commercial office project for Argent LLP at the King's Cross development site in London.[3] SCP was engaged at RIBA stage 2 to provide carbon analysis advice across all areas of design for the duration of the project. At stage 2, SCP provided detailed life cycle and carbon emissions analysis of the various cladding and structure options under consideration.

Facade systems can typically account for a significant proportion of a building's embodied carbon (13-21% range; average 16%) and construction costs (17-22% range; average 19%) at practical completion.

Additionally, the specification and procurement of a building's facade can have a long lead-time (40-plus weeks is typical). This can limit flexibility, so early discussions and decisions around low carbon facade options are important.

Aluminium, a commonly used facade material, has a highly energy-intensive production process and is responsible for around 1% of global greenhouse gas emissions. However, since the carbon intensity of aluminium can vary 20-fold (from virgin to recycled aluminium), the embodied carbon of aluminium components can be greatly reduced through some simple design and specification decisions.

The global consumption of aluminium is expected to triple or quadruple by 2050 and, while the rate of recycling can be improved (approximately 30% of aluminium in circulation is recycled), much of this demand will need to be met through carbon-intensive virgin aluminium. Within Europe, 65% of the aluminium consumed is produced outside the EU Emissions Trading System, so it is important to consider the global aluminium supply chain. Figure 2.10 maps out an illustrative example of virgin aluminium production: Bauxite (labelled 1 in figure 2.10) is extracted from a mine in Brazil and transported by road to a refinery where it is converted to alumina (2). The alumina is shipped to a plant in Norway where it is smelted into aluminium billets (3) via an electrolytic process. The billets are transported to Germany where they are extruded (4) into profiles. These are then anodised (5) in England before being fabricated (6) into curtain wall frames in Northern Ireland. Finally, the frames are delivered to the construction site in London (7).

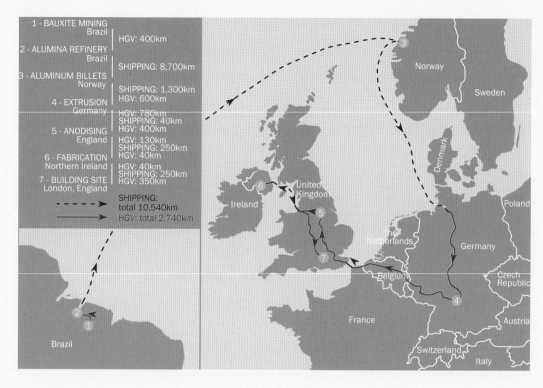

Figure 2.10: Illustrative supply chain for aluminium curtain wall frame.

The most significant step from a carbon perspective is the electrolytic smelting process, which uses a large amount of electricity and accounts for around 60-90% of emissions. The location of the smelting plant, and consequently the mix of energy sources of the electricity used, is therefore a key negative emissions factor. The energy mix can range from coal-dominated (80% coal in China – the world's largest producer of virgin aluminium, representing a third of global supply) to renewable-dominated (90% hydroelectric in Latin America). The careful selection of an aluminium supplier (in terms of recycled content and energy source) can greatly reduce the embodied carbon of the purchased product. This 'green demand' can also provide a market signal to aluminium producers and incentivise investment in low carbon production technologies, recycling and the circular economy, thus helping to drive the decarbonisation of the aluminium sector in the long term.

The effect of some common specification and procurement choices on the embodied carbon of 1kg of aluminium is shown in figure 2.11. One of the simplest ways to reduce aluminium's embodied carbon is to use aluminium with a higher recycled content. Compared with virgin aluminium, increasing the proportion of recycled content can reduce the embodied carbon by around 42% for medium recycled content (50% recycled), or by 75% for very high recycled content (90% recycled). Sourcing aluminium produced using renewable hydro-energy (rather than a conventional energy mix) can reduce embodied carbon by 25%.

Finally, the choice of aluminium finish will alter the embodied carbon, but this may affect the appearance. A polyester powder coated (PPC) finish can save up to about 30% embodied carbon compared with an anodised finish. Some large paint manufacturers now offer an 'anodised look' PPC finish, which offers much lower embodied carbon without compromising the aesthetic. The finish also affects recyclability at end of life. Anodising aluminium changes its chemistry and makes it more expensive and complex to recycle than a PPC finish. Therefore, anyone following circular economy principles would do well to avoid anodising aluminium.

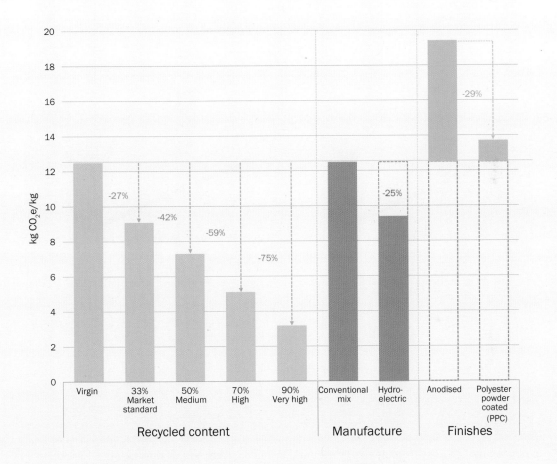

Figure 2.11: Embodied carbon of 1kg aluminium (BS EN 15978:2011, module A1-A3).

Timber/composite frames

An effective way to reduce the embodied carbon of a curtain wall frame is to move away from a fully aluminium construction to a composite aluminium and timber frame. Timber has considerably lower embodied carbon than aluminium and has the benefit of carbon sequestration during tree growth. However, it is important to note firstly that this composite material should be easy to separate, and secondly that the timber should be disposed of appropriately at end of life (recycling, reuse, or combustion for energy or heat). If the timber is sent to landfill, the subsequent methane emitted during decomposition can negate much of the carbon benefits that timber offers.

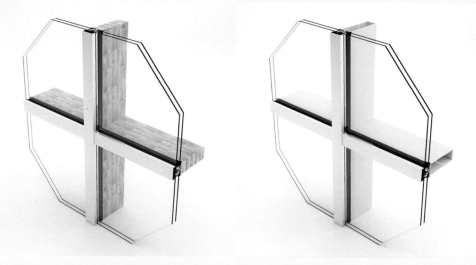

Figure 2.12: Curtain walling types – composite aluminium timber frame (right) and aluminium (left).

Curtain wall systems – WLC analysis

The WLC per m² of façade for the worst case scenario – fully anodised, virgin aluminium frame produced using a conventional energy mix, and including glass, gaskets, fixings, etc – is shown on the left of figure 2.13. The potential percentage reduction in WLC for each measure is shown in turn, starting with the energy source, then the aluminium frame finish, the recycled content of the aluminium, and finally the option of a composite (aluminium timber) frame. The far right of the diagram shows the WLC of the best case scenario: a composite frame with highly recycled, PPC-finished aluminium produced using renewable energy.

If the appearance of the facade cannot be changed, the WLC can still be reduced by 54% against the worst case. Our analysis shows that 10% of this reduction comes from sourcing hydro-produced aluminium, 17% from specifying a PPC finish with an anodised look instead of an anodised finish, and a further 27% is achieved by using aluminium with 90% recycled content.

If the appearance can be changed, specifying a composite aluminium timber frame provides a further 17% saving, giving a total WLC reduction of 71% against the worst case scenario.

This analysis shows that these reductions are not marginal, and that big improvements can be made through a thorough understanding of the environmental consequences of aesthetic design decisions. These can also have direct financial benefits, as PPC on aluminium with high recycled content is usually significantly cheaper than anodising predominantly virgin aluminium extrusions.

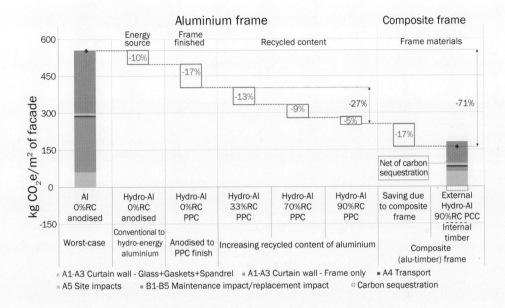

Figure 2.13: The effect of low carbon choices on the whole life carbon of a facade system.

Curtain wall systems – life cycle and other considerations

Typically, the life cycle of traditional aluminium curtain walling is limited to about 40-50 years. The principal reasons are that the seals to the double- (or triple-) glazed units fail, the finishes (particularly powder coating) deteriorate and the neoprene gaskets need replacing. Some of these failures are accentuated by the orientation and location of the building. Knowledge and consideration of the lifespan aspects of such systems should be included in design thinking from the outset. The components of any such system will deteriorate at different rates; thus a system is usually dependent on the item with the shortest life expectancy, ie the 'weakest link'. Examining the comparative life cycles of the various components in a system such as a facade is therefore crucial to its overall life expectancy.

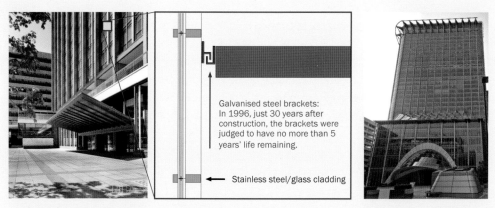

Figure 2.14: Stainless steel/glass cladding – Britannic House, London. Illustrating that the life of a system is dependent on the weakest link.

Galvanised steel brackets:
In 1996, just 30 years after construction, the brackets were judged to have no more than 5 years' life remaining.

← Stainless steel/glass cladding

The above example shows the original Britannic House, built in 1967 with stainless steel cladding. This had a potentially unlimited lifespan except that, crucially, the stainless steel cladding was held to the structure with galvanised fixings that needed replacing by 1996. This led to a full cladding replacement and remodelling by architects Sheppard Robson. Fortunately, the concrete frame was retained and reused.

Cladding maintenance and replacement life cycles should be considered in relation to the maintenance/replacement cycles of other systems within the building, and in relation to the activities of the occupants (eg lease cycles). Construction methodology also has an impact on life cycle. Unitised cladding systems, which are interlocking across a facade, make local change or upgrading very difficult, if not impossible. The ability to maintain and/or to dismantle a facade easily and efficiently is a low carbon characteristic. A final positive life cycle attribute is designing in the ability to recycle or even fully reuse a facade. Other factors to consider that could reduce the WLC footprint include high road transport emissions associated with heavy glazing elements; using local sources will reduce emissions and provide social benefits local to the site.

Conclusions

The most significant factors with respect to the carbon footprint of aluminium used in curtain walling are recycled content and surface finish. Most cladding manufacturers use a proportion of recycled content, but this can vary considerably – by up to as much as 80-90%. It is worth asking for this information as part of the tender process. Where the recycled content is sourced also influences the transport emissions.

Typically powder coating has lower initial carbon costs in comparison with anodising; however, finish life expectancy should also be considered when making a choice.

Anodising requires more consistent and therefore higher quality aluminium to ensure a consistent colour, whereas powder coating does not. This can affect price. Each finishing process has different energy demands and chemical impacts. The key point is to be aware of these impacts when making choices.

3

Recycling, reuse and the circular economy

Overview

A circular economy is defined by the Ellen MacArthur Foundation thus:

...restorative and regenerative by design, and aims to keep products, components and materials at their highest utility and value at all times. The concept distinguishes between technical and biological cycles.[1]

For more information see the Ellen MacArthur website, which covers the circular economy in excellent detail.

In the built environment, an analysis of the carbon impacts of reuse and recycling in comparison to the use of new material helps to quantify the benefits of circular economic thinking. A fundamental principle of a low carbon, circular economy should be to maximise beneficial recycling wherever possible. Circularity has two principle low carbon benefits: firstly, reducing waste; secondly, reducing the need for new materials.

Recycling can occur at any scale, from reuse of entire structures and buildings (as in refurbishment or retrofit projects) through reuse of systems to recycling individual components or materials. The ideal is for a recycled item to be reused at the highest possible level. A brick can be reused as a brick, which removes the need to make a new brick, or it can become ballast in a foundation, where its carbon value is lower. Continuing with the brick example, very strong mortar is all but impossible to remove from bricks, whereas a softer mortar makes them relatively easy to reuse. This illustrates the importance of forward thinking to end of life at the design stage. Recycling is a two-way thought process: not only should we be designing to use the maximum recycled material, we should also be doing so in such a way as to enable future recycling of our buildings whole or as components with minimum waste and use of energy.

A traditional linear economy involves sourcing new raw material, making it into products, using those products, and then treating the redundant products as waste. This is profligate, inefficient and unsustainable in the long term. Far better is for a waste product to be reused to form a new product using a minimum of new material and energy. Confusingly, it is possible to use recycled material and still increase the carbon footprint of a building. This occurs where, for example, recycled materials are transported long distances, or where energy-intensive reworking of waste material is required. It is therefore essential when considering the use of recycled material to achieve a full understanding and quantification of its sourcing, fabrication, delivery and ultimate disposal.

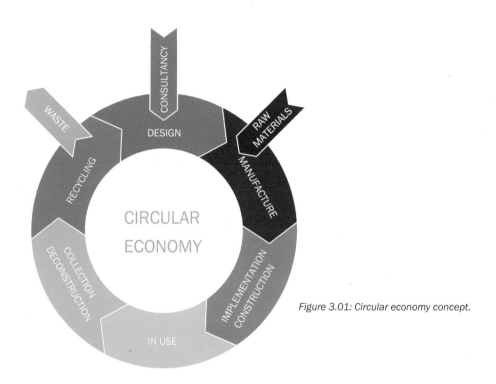

Figure 3.01: Circular economy concept.

Reuse and existing buildings

With respect to the built environment, the optimum is to reuse as much existing structure and material as possible, preferably without the carbon costs of dismantling and relocation. This was previously known by the unappealing title of refurbishment, but is now called retrofit. Retrofit involves updating existing systems with new, performance-enhancing additions; used in relation to buildings, it implies a refurbishment that has an additional 'green' tinge, including energy-efficient and/or low carbon measures that are over and above the basic Building Regulations requirements.

The vast majority of building work in the UK involves the reuse of existing buildings. The retained embodied carbon (ie emissions already released through earlier construction activity) avoids the need for new equivalent construction. Retention and refurbishment of existing buildings has many benefits compared to equivalent new build, including cost of construction, programme to delivery, and often localism and social benefits. The problem is that where there is a choice, refurbishment/retrofit is often perceived as the less desirable option from both environmental and commercial perspectives. It is not unusual for the case for demolishing and replacing existing older buildings to include the claim that they are poor environmental performers and, in emissions terms, better replaced with new. Case study 3 suggests that this is not necessarily true.

The 2012 abolition of VAT relief on listed buildings, and the fact that VAT is generally applied at the standard rate to retrofit (compared to zero-rated new build) further disadvantages the potential for retaining and recycling older buildings. In general, the carbon, environmental and long-term economic value of existing structure and fabric is not properly considered. From an environmental performance perspective, existing buildings are usually judged solely on their operational carbon emissions costs, and in direct comparison with an equivalent new build the retrofit will typically not perform as well.

However, taking a whole life carbon emissions approach, where both operational and embodied carbon emissions costs are assessed, you get a different picture. Case study 3 illustrates the carbon benefits of a high-quality retrofit in comparison to an equivalent high-performance new build to Passivhaus standards. In this example, the retrofit performs better in whole life carbon terms due to the retained embodied carbon.

The opportunities for retrofit are restricted when it comes to listed buildings or conservation areas. This is due to understandable concern about the impact of retrofit measures on the historic nature of the fabric, and the potential for damage due to poorly thought-through insulation, airtightness, etc. However, the long-term social and economic value of such properties – on which their ultimate existence relies – suggests that maintaining the status quo is not an option. To ensure their continued value to society, methods must be developed to ensure listed buildings get closer to current new-build environmental standards. The National Trust for England and Wales has committed to reducing its dependence on fossil fuels by 50% by 2020, and the National Trust for Scotland likewise 45% by 2020. The action of these leading heritage organisations suggests that there is scope to improve the operational performance of even the most sensitive historic buildings. Case study 4 examines the whole life carbon emissions impacts of different standards of retrofit. This case study shows that, despite their associated embodied costs, additional physical measures provide worthwhile operational and whole life carbon benefits.

Case studies 3 and 4 suggest that UK government policy aimed at reducing carbon emissions in the built environment should be strongly geared to encouraging retrofit, and to the highest standards. If we are to move towards a circular economy, then we need to start with improving how we reuse existing buildings. This has long-term economic and environmental benefits. However, it would require the VAT regime for retrofit to be brought into line with new build, and, in the case of listed buildings, methods must be developed to enable significant improvement in their environmental performance.

It is worth noting that whole life carbon analysis combined with life cycle analysis can greatly improve our understanding of the environmental and financial impacts of various retrofit strategies. (See also the sections on carbon cost analysis and MAC curves in Chapter 6.)

Future circularity

The quest for a truly zero carbon future has focused thinking on how buildings are made, where they come from and how they are disposed of. It is said that in nature there is no waste – in other words, there is total resource-efficiency. The current cycle of making, using and disposing of buildings is entirely counter to this principle. If we are to move on to a truly zero carbon trajectory for the life of buildings, then we must change the way we make them, and optimise the use of recycled material as a matter of course. We must think of a building as an evolving process rather than a box that is 'finished' at a fixed point in time.

Future low carbon buildings will be made of components that are close to 100% recyclable either directly by reusing them as is, or indirectly – as my colleague Dr Qian Li says, 'Use what you have to make what you will have.' Architects and engineers will, from the outset, have to design with consideration for the future life of materials and components and not just in response to their immediate brief. Waste from everyday consumables will be used both to manufacture building materials and to power the fabrication process. Total flexibility will be fundamental: buildings will be capable of being changed, dismantled, moved and reassembled with the minimum addition of new resources and energy. This is essentially an updated version of the 1970s concept coined by former president of the RIBA, Sir Alex Gordon: 'Long life, loose fit, low energy.'[2]

However, the buildings resulting from this particular approach were typically products of a linear economy, and produced the waste associated with such fabrication processes. Taking a more circular approach, the ideal is to both design with reuse and design for reuse. The additional development of nonlinear processes (eg 3D printing and self-assembly) will potentially deliver both resource optimisation and zero waste, and will directly reduce the carbon emissions cost of making buildings.

Reuse of resources is not a new concept. Making buildings out of redundant material or trash, while not routine, is certainly not unheard of. Typically, though, such buildings or constructions have been associated with alternative living, ie not seen as mainstream or commercially viable. Recycling of basic materials is, however, much more widespread, occurring in a large range of construction materials such as steel, aluminium, concrete (cement replacements) and so on. What is rarer is the idea of designing buildings to be capable of total reuse without waste or complex reworking.

A feature of the circular economy as applied to buildings is the idea of them being inherently flexible and reusable, not just as a whole but as a collection of materials. For any organisation occupying a building, there is almost always the need to adapt even the most carefully bespoke building to meet changing circumstances. Our current approach to change typically entails destruction followed by new construction, whether it is through alterations to interior layout or the creation of additional space. A building can be seen as an assembly of materials and systems that need to be capable of random and easy change. For many large organisations, change is inevitable but is usually seen as an irritant and a necessary evil. If changes were easier, less wasteful, and inherently democratic, this could well turn building change from a negative to a positive. This would require bringing together some of the above ideas, and enabling people to drive change themselves. To do this, we need to harness the collective intelligence of the building users. A simple illustration of human/product interface is artificial intelligence beer: this beer responds to consumers through social media to change its ingredients and improve its taste.

A similar example of the power of collective thought is the termite mound. Termites individually know very little, but collectively they design and build termite mounds that ensure that the queen located in the centre is kept at a precise temperature. They do this by using their own version of 3D printing (sand mixed with saliva) to collectively produce mounds with highly sophisticated passive cooling, heat rejection and ventilation systems.

Could the collective intelligence of humans be channelled into improving and adapting their immediate environment? Google recently bought the British company DeepMind, which specialises in the human/AI interface. Linking this concept with digital mapping, designing for reuse, 3D printing, etc might enable buildings that could be designed by the occupants. A simple example of this would be to monitor individual tolerance to temperature over a whole group within a room, with the temperature adjusted by the average requirement. If the activity within the room changed from passive to active, the room temperature would change to meet the new circumstances. In fact, Google already markets an intelligent temperature control product called Nest. Nest learns the occupier's behaviour, even automatically turning down the temperature when the house is empty. This of course helps reduce energy wastage.

Imagine if the requirement were changed from temperature to the need for a new meeting room and add in reuse of materials, etc. The following diagrams show the carbon activity of creating a new space. The first shows the current energy and material transaction associated with making a new room: the old and new are entirely separate, with the old being 100% waste. The proposed energy and material transaction shows the new being fabricated using the old, with the process powered by food and other material waste. The final diagram shows the carbon activity associated with making a new meeting room using redundant material from a building or group of buildings large enough to support this process.

Energy and material transaction - current

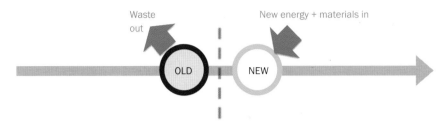

Figure 3.02: This diagram represents a normal building alteration, with the old becoming all waste, and the new is from entirely new resources. There is no connection between the two.

Energy and material transaction - proposed

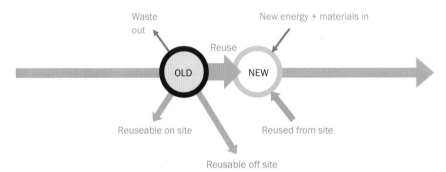

Figure 3.03: This diagram is the most 'circular' approach with resources managed to reduce waste and optimise reuse.

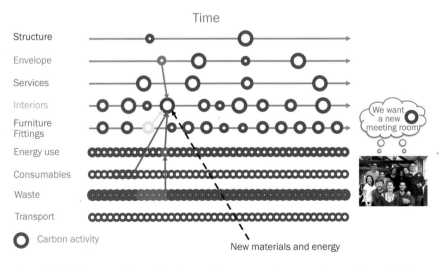

Figure 3.04: Carbon map illustrating the possible sources of energy and materials required to create a new space.

This approach requires tracking and mobilising all material-related data within a building or group of buildings and using this as a conduit to facilitate and optimise change. This is likely to be a future, active version of BIM that interacts with AI, digital space mapping and localised product manufacture. Aggregating the previous diagram produces the following conceptual carbon activity matrix:

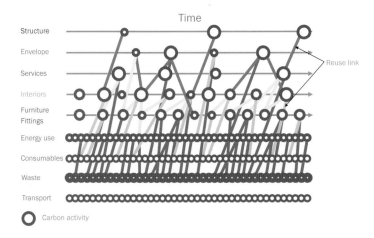

Figure 3.05: Carbon activity map – recycling from within. Extrapolating from 3.04, this shows how energy and materials might flow around a large building or group of buildings over time.

This illustrates the idea of the building as an organism that undertakes change in response to occupier requirements. It feeds off itself, ie redundant material, waste from food and other consumables, and also from surrounding buildings. It is potentially a highly resource-efficient process. And while I have suggested that this ultra-low carbon future is the product of sophisticated technology, the above diagram could just as well apply to a group of buildings built entirely from timber. The essence is the ability to reuse and interchange objects in response to user requirements without waste and with the minimum of CO_2e emissions.

Waste material from day-to-day building use can be used to make building components, or to provide the energy to do so. The quantity of waste material that western societies produce is truly phenomenal. A large proportion already goes to recycling depots for reuse, although often to be used at a lower level. Much goes to power generation. The ideal is to pre-empt this process by enabling localised energy generation and even production.

The circular economy principle is also inherent in rethinking procurement to optimise reuse and improve market incentives. An example of this is an area of new lighting at Schiphol Airport in Amsterdam. The traditional route would involve employing an MEP engineer to lay out and specify the lighting requirements. This is then tendered by the supply chain where the incentive is to produce the cheapest light fitting to win the job. The circular approach is to 'buy light' rather than light fittings. The supply chain is asked to tender to provide an illumination level for a given period, say 20 years. The tenderer is incentivised to choose the minimum number of fittings to achieve this and, as he or she retains ownership of the fittings, to also provide a more durable fitting to increase life expectancy and minimise replacement, and one that has value when no longer required. Additionally, fewer maintenance visits equals less fuel use. Anglian Water is another innovator in this area, believing that reducing carbon costs also reduces financial costs. For example, Anglian Water now asks the supply chain to 'move water' rather than to provide a pre-determined pumping building. This encourages innovation and reduces procurement costs.

Building designers need to be made aware of the importance of carbon reduction, and to adjust working practices and methods to facilitate it. Material selection, project detailing/ structural calculations, and thinking long-term past practical completion can all aid dismantling, recycling and reuse, and reduce carbon emissions.

Are today's building designers equipped to design zero carbon buildings? The basic processes for truly zero carbon assembly, enabling 100% reuse and using predominantly recycled material, will be highly sophisticated. Advanced product designers and intelligent software may be required to track and manage large amounts of materials data. Efficiencies of scale, as in city-wide material trading, will be needed. The internet can obviously facilitate this; however, the demand for recycled material as opposed to new is not yet a fully economic proposition in a number of cases. Work being carried out with Grosvenor, which owns more than 6,000 properties in London, suggests that even where there is the will to recycle, tracking and valuing reusable materials (bricks, timber, aggregate, etc) for potential reuse is a major challenge, and is often more expensive than buying new.

Real and imagined cost concerns as well as the potential unpredictability of supply are undoubtedly major impediments to recycling and the circular economic principle with respect to design and construction. But this can be changed. On several campus-type projects (eg Gatwick, Warwick University) involving large numbers of buildings that are prone to change and churn, the idea of buildings designed from the outset to be capable of easy change, extension, reuse and relocation to meet different demands is being actively considered. With the aid of 'big data' tracking, this will enable the next generation of buildings to be made from the current with known cost, supply and risk profiles (see case study 5: Circularity in practice – relocating a 3500m^2 building). Using the internet to bring supply and demand much closer together will help facilitate this kind of approach at the city-wide scale.

Demand for recycled materials and products needs to start with clients, investors and occupiers. This will only happen with increased awareness of the benefits, reduced risk and a clear need for lower whole life carbon buildings. For designers, contractors and the supply chain, education is also necessary to bring about increased understanding of recycling and the circular economy concept.

CASE STUDY 3:

Carbon benefits of retrofit vs new build

BY CHRISTINA STUART

This case study, undertaken in 2013, looks at the carbon benefits of recycling whole buildings in comparison to the highest environmental quality new build, and is based on project work done for Grosvenor in London.[3] Specifically, it compares three residential scenarios over a 60-year period, as follows:

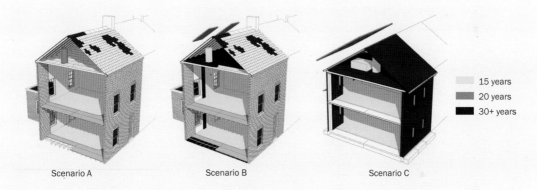

	15 years
	20 years
	30+ years

Scenario A   Scenario B   Scenario C

Figure 3.06: Residential scenarios over a 60-year period, see below.

Scenario A
The baseline is a two-storey, 19th-century, brick terraced house with a slate pitched roof and a flat roof extension to the rear – typical of much urban housing in Britain. No work beyond basic maintenance and decoration is assumed.

Scenario B
Retrofit of the baseline building is the second option. This takes a comprehensive, 'fabric first' approach to improving building envelope and the operational performance, while maintaining the vapour permeability of the original construction. The house is in a conservation area, ruling out measures such as external wall insulation to the rear of the property, but solar photovoltaic panels (PVs), airtightness and mechanical ventilation heat recovery are proposed.

Scenario C

The last option is the replacement of the existing building with an exemplar new building. The house is insulated to the Passivhaus standard and is zero carbon, as defined by the UK government's 2016 target for new homes (all regulated operational carbon is offset by 25m² solar PVs). The substructure is concrete. The frame, wall cladding and roof are all timber.

The detailed assumptions are as follows:

		Scenario A	Scenario B	Scenario C
	Area (NIA)	112m²	108m²	115m²
Construction	Facade	Two skin brick and plaster	150mm wood fibre internal wall insulation. General draught proofing	Timber frame, larch cladding and 250mm cellulose wall insulation
	Ground	Suspended timber floors	150mm hemp insulation laid between floor joists	Concrete foundations and 240mm polystyrene insulation
	Windows	Leaky sash and case windows	Slimline double-glazed sash and case windows	Triple-glazed timber windows
	Roof	Pitched slate roof. Flat roof extension to garden	300mm mineral wool insulation between rafters	540mm cellulose roof insulation. Larch tiles
	Services	Wet central heating system run off old gas boiler	Combi boiler, LED lighting and MVHR	Combi boiler and MVHR
	Renewables	None	3m² solar PVs	25m² solar PVs
	Airtightness	Very poor	Improved	Very high
	Other	Minor decoration	Major redecoration associated with works	Demolition of existing and waste transport
Construction costs (£/m²) at practical completion*		50	500	1750
Dwelling emission rate (kg CO_2/m²)**		72.8	21.6	0

Table 3.01: Assumptions for residential scenarios.
Source: SCP (Christina Stuart)

Findings

As can be seen below, there are considerable differences between the whole life carbon of the three options.

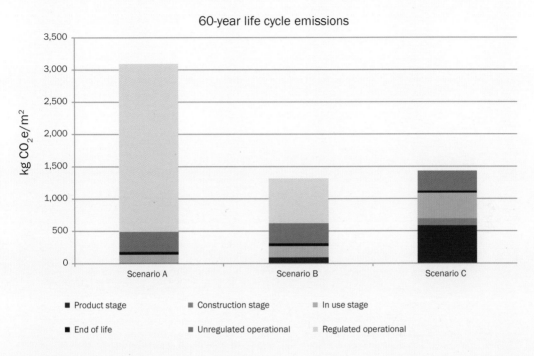

Figure 3.07: Whole life carbon scenarios, see below.

- The baseline scenario A's whole life carbon emissions over 60 years is double that of the other scenarios. With very little capital carbon expenditure, almost all the emissions are operational.
- Scenario B shows that it is possible to make substantial reductions in emissions through retrofit – though the operational performance is obviously still well below Passivhaus standards.
- The additional embodied carbon required for installing and maintaining the retrofit measures is less than 150kg CO_2e/m^2. This carbon expenditure effectively halves the whole life emissions through operational savings. This carbon return supports retrofit investment as an 'allowable solution' for offsetting emissions.
- The life cycle analysis suggests scenarios B and C are similar over 60 years, but the whole life costs of B are slightly better than C.
- The key difference between the retrofit and rebuild whole life carbon is the ratio of operational to embodied emissions, with the 80/20% split reversed in scenarios B and C.

- In the Passivhaus scenario, most emissions beyond practical completion are due to replacement of elements such as solar panels and cladding. This is partly because renewal of items would likely bring forward the replacement of connected elements, eg timber cladding would probably be replaced at the same time as cellulose insulation. Scenario C has significantly more PVs than B, with attendant embodied costs of replacement.
- Over the long term, the emissions of the unimproved house increase more rapidly than the other options due to its larger operational demand.
- This is also due to heavier reliance on gas, which is more efficient in the short term but less so as the grid decarbonises. It may therefore be appropriate to change the heating and hot water systems to electricity in the medium term.

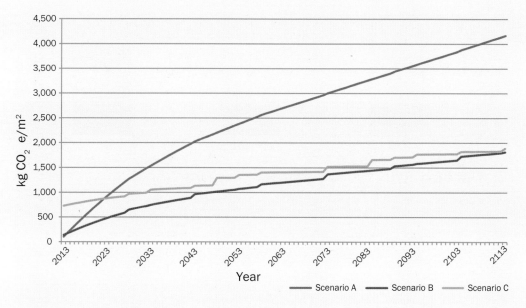

Figure 3.08: Future prediction of embodied carbon scenarios.

- As shown in the diagram above, Scenario B has the lowest whole life carbon in 2050. This suggests that retrofit is the best strategy for reducing emissions by this date in order to mitigate climate change.
- As it does not benefit from retained fabric, the whole life carbon footprint of scenario C is significantly higher at practical completion, reflecting the embodied carbon in demolition, materials and all-new construction.
- The gap narrows between scenarios B and C, with the Passivhaus performing better than the retrofit after 100 years.

- However, while the materials in the new build are green, they may be less durable than traditional construction (the emissions from which have already been expended). This would warrant a higher maintenance cost over time. Alternatively, use of more durable materials (eg brick cladding) would reduce whole life maintenance carbon costs, but increase the initial carbon cost of construction.
- Low house-building rates make it likely that most houses in 2050 already exist today. Therefore, the biggest gains are to be made in improving the energy efficiency of our existing building stock. Currently fewer than 5% of solid walls have some form of insulation, in contrast to 61% of cavity walls.

Assumptions

- Sequestration – the absorption of carbon dioxide by plants and trees – is outside the scope of BS EN 15978. The benefit may have already been claimed by producers, and varies depending on factors such as tree type, growth rate, processing, and treatment of waste. The whole life carbon of scenario C would be reduced by about 11% over 60 years if sequestration was included for the timber frame.
- It was assumed that 25% of construction waste would be sent to landfill, increasing end of life carbon emissions for organic materials such as timber and cellulose insulation. This figure is attributed to the timber in the product stage, for the reasons outlined above, but if separated would increase the end of life stage, particularly for scenario C.
- Allowance was made for 92% grid decarbonisation by 2045.[4] Plant efficiency is assumed to improve by 20% per replacement.
- Unregulated operational emissions from items such as cookers and televisions were kept constant across all three scenarios. These depend on occupant behaviour and efficiency of appliances, so would likely be smaller for scenario C as all the fittings would be new.
- The impact of projected climate change on demand for heating and cooling has not been included. For some of the issues involved, refer to SCP's 2011 real estate climate change model for the RICS,[5] and SCP's Climatic Risk Toolkit for the RICS 2015.[6]

Conclusions

This case study highlights the importance taking a holistic, whole life view of carbon emissions, and specifically the crucial role of retrofit in the UK achieving a low carbon future. There are of course economic and social arguments for building new housing; however, the overall impact of intelligent retrofit is likely to be far more significant to the UK's carbon footprint than improving the way we build new buildings. Going up a notch with respect to retrofit, PassivHaus EnerPhit variant will undoubtedly perform better than most new buildings from a whole life perspective, and such exemplar development should be encouraged. The only provisos would be to minimise embodied costs and consider the life cycle aspects when building to new Passivhaus standards.

CASE STUDY 4:
Retrofit – EnerPHit v Part L
BY PRIYANKA ARORA AND MAIIA WILLIAMS

This case study is based on work done for Grosvenor on its London estate (Belgravia and Mayfair). It was initially published in *Building* magazine[7] but has been adapted for inclusion in this book.

In 2015, following the work in case study 3, a more detailed comparative exercise of retrofitting was undertaken, specifically focusing on the Passivhaus EnerPHit standard. EnerPHit is the highest energy standard for refurbishments in the UK and is based on the German Passivhaus quality-approved certification criteria. Broadly speaking, it means that the property is virtually airtight and has high insulation levels, resulting in a very low heating demand – hence the term passive. This is achieved with limited intervention to the existing building and without excessive costs.

This case study compares three scenarios from the whole life carbon perspective:

Scenario 1: a typical un-refurbished terrace;

Scenario 2: a Part L-compliant retrofit;

Scenario 3: a deep retrofit to EnerPHit standards. This has been shown with and without PVs to illustrate the impact of renewables in this case.

Building to EnerPHit standards puts additional pressure on the design team and the contractor as the requirements are specific and can be considered more demanding than standard Part L-compliant retrofit. Experience show that while this may be the initial impression, the solution lies in additional training of the project team, and ensuring that the retrofit works by the contractor are to the highest quality standard. Once the contractor is fully trained and understands what is required, experience shows that they rise to the challenge. The principal benefits of EnerPHit are low energy bills,[8] improved comfort, better sound insulation, no internal condensation, improved health, and higher quality control during construction.[9]

Scenarios explained

Element	Scenario 1: Un-refurbished terrace	Scenario 2: Part L-compliant retrofit	Scenario 3: Deep retrofit to EnerPHit standard
Building envelope	Solid brick	Solid brick with 20mm internal breathable aerogel insulation (0.50W/m^2.K) to front and external insulation with brick slips to rear facade (0.30W/m^2.K)	Solid brick with 70mm internal breathable aerogel insulation (0.15W/m^2.K) to front and external insulation with brick slips to rear facade (0.15W/m^2.K)
Ground floor	Existing floor, no insulation	125mm PIR insulation	175mm PIR insulation (0.15W/m^2.K) Cellular glass insulation around steel beams and thresholds to avoid cold bridges
Windows	Single-glazed sash windows	Double-glazed sash windows	Triple-glazed mock sash windows
Roof	Existing timber roof, <100mm insulation	200mm mineral wool insulation between rafters	200mm mineral wool between rafters +100mm PIR insulation above
Renewables	None	None	9 m^2 PV panels
Heating	Old inefficient gas boiler + radiators	New efficient condensing boiler + radiators	New efficient condensing boiler (small demand) + radiators
Ventilation	Manual-opening windows	Manual-opening windows	MVHR + manual-opening windows
Airtightness	Very poor (15-35 m^3/m^2.h@50Pa)	Improved (15 m^3/m^2.h@50Pa)	Very high (0.7 m^3/m^2.h@50Pa)
DER* operational (kg CO_2e/m^2)	94	40	12 excl. PVs (0 incl. PVs)
WLC (kg CO_2e/ m^2)	4940	3100	1870 excl. PVs (1820 incl. PVs)

DER based on SAP calculations from real project data from Grosvenor Britain and Ireland

Table 3.02: EnerPHit v Part L scenarios.
Source: SCP (Maiia Williams, Priyanka Arora)

Scenario 1 DECC Average Annual Domestic Gas Bills 2014: https://www.gov.uk/government/ statistical-data-sets/annual-domestic- energy-price-statistics
Scenario 2 D. Johnson, D. Farmer, M. Brooke-Peat & D. Miles-Shenton 'Bridging the domestic building fabric performance gap', 2014, Leeds Beckett Repository.
Scenario 3 DER based on SAP calculations from real project data from Grosvenor Britain and Ireland.

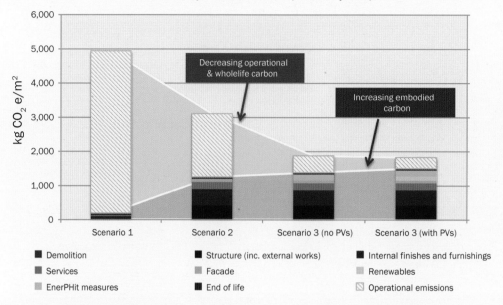

Figure 3.09: Whole life carbon assessment over 60 years.

The graph above shows considerable differences between the whole life carbon footprints of the three scenarios over 60 years. The operational emissions decrease steeply with each successive measure; however, the increase in embodied carbon after the first jump is relatively gradual.

As you would expect, scenario 2 (Part L retrofit) shows the operational energy (carbon) costs reduced by some 60% compared to that of the un-refurbished property, but at a significant embodied cost. In overall whole life carbon terms, the reduction is more like 40%.

However, scenario 3 (EnerPHit standard) shows that, for comparatively little additional embodied cost, you get a very significant additional operational saving. Compare the EnerPHit cost with the reduction in operational energy between scenarios 2 and 3. The final bar shows EnerPHit with the embodied costs and the operational energy savings of introducing PVs. This leads to a further slight improvement.

Assumptions

This study assumes no demolition waste to landfill, 50% waste recycled on site, timber sequestration excluded, grid decarbonisation allowed for, and no allowance of climate change impact on heating demand.

Conclusions

- Deep retrofit to EnerPHit standard offers better overall carbon efficiency compared to the Part L retrofit, achieving 40% whole life carbon savings. Increasing embodied carbon costs through additional insulation, providing airtightness, etc, can be justified by greater operational carbon savings.
- Thin, but expensive, internal insulation systems may be justifiable in high value or heritage buildings, whereas less expensive external systems are likely to be more appropriate for upgrading lower value properties.
- As much as 75% improvement in operational energy performance can be achieved by as little as 8% increase in insulation costs to upgrade from Part L compliance to EnerPHit standards.
- Use of photovoltaic panels to provide electricity is just about justifiable in carbon emissions terms; however, the economic benefits may be less clear.
- Experience shows that achieving EnerPHit standard upgrades to many property types, including heritage assets, is a carbon-efficient way forward.

CASE STUDY 5:

Circularity in practice – relocating a 3500m² building

BY SIMON STURGIS

This project, completed in 2013, demonstrates the environmental and financial benefits of circular economic thinking. The client, SEGRO, owned a 3500m² office and warehouse that was ten years old and recently vacated in Leigh Road, Slough, England. The building was not letting, but there was a demand for a similar building 2km away in Cambridge Avenue. The initial thought had been to demolish and dispose of the original building and build a new one in Cambridge Avenue. Following initial carbon-related advice, the client decided to reduce the carbon impacts by dismantling, moving and reassembling the building in the new location. This case study is a carbon and financial comparison between the recycled building and an identical new building.

Original building

The Leigh Road building is a typical out-of-town building: concrete foundations and ground slab, steel frame with ribdeck and concrete first floor, aluminium and glass cladding, insulated metal deck roof. The two-storey office areas are standard, basic fitout, raised floors and suspended ceilings, modular light fittings and fancoil cooling system. There are stairs and a lift connecting the two office levels, with toilets on both floors.

Relocated building

The team undertook a detailed examination to see what could be economically recycled. In total, some 70% of the original material was reused, including the steel frame, the cladding, the lift, most of the services and the roof deck. Most concrete needed replacing, as did subsurface drainage and foundations, and roof finish.

Figure 3.10: Recycling buildings – relocated and completed building.

Figure 3.11: Recycling buildings – structural frame.

Cost and carbon saving*

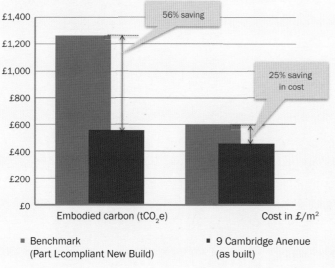

* excluding external works

Figure 3.12: Recycling buildings – savings.

Conclusions

As noted, 70% of material was reused, with a reduced carbon cost compared with an identical new build of some 40%. In addition, the building was 25% cheaper than a new build. The programme for either solution was about the same but, as the lift assembly was being reused, the normal long lead time did not arise. It should be noted that all of this was achieved with a building not originally designed for reuse. It can be reasonably assumed that designing a building specifically for such reuse would only improve on the above figures. The lessons learned from this case study can be applied not only to buildings such as this but also buildings that are likely to require partial change and adaptation over their life.

The building typology in this case study is typical of a large number of out-of-town uses, including retail, industrial units and many more. These are found in all countries as they are cheap and simple to build. The life expectancy is generally very short – often no more than 20 years for retail – after which the structure and fabric are typically trashed, at best for basic recycling. This involves significant energy use to refabricate the base material into new components. This cannot be the optimum use of resources. How much better it would be if the building were designed as a collection of reusable components that would have a value at the end of their initial life. Most of these buildings are effectively modular and therefore, with modest adaptation, capable of joining the circular economy.

CASE STUDY 6:

Recycling out-of-town shopping centres

BY SIMON STURGIS AND QIAN LI

This case study is based on a 30,000m² shopping centre in Hampshire owned by British Land. What is of interest is the life cycle over the next 60 years, and what lessons this holds for the present. The study is based on the practical lessons learned and data gathered in case study 5, and projecting into the future different commercial scenarios. The study only looks the buildings in isolation. These developments are typically very poor in terms of overall carbon footprint due to their out-of-town location and substantial car parking provision, and all that entails in both material and significant consumer fuel usage.

The new scheme consists of double-storey retail shells capable of extensive subdivision and includes landscaping and car parking. It is built to a high standard of quality and represents the forefront of a contemporary approach to sustainability, achieving BREEAM Excellent, and including PVs. The buildings consist of steel frames with in situ concrete slabs, insulated roof deck, and double- and triple-height glazing with oak-faced cladding. The subdivision walls are a stud wall system.

The developer has a detailed sustainability policy, including an environmental site management system to ISO 14001, procedures to minimise ground and surface water pollution, and measures to manage water, waste and energy use during the construction process.

This study considers three possible future scenarios for the shopping centre in whole life carbon terms. This is split into the construction phase to practical completion, and the whole life phase, which covers the initial construction and the life of the centre over the 60-year period. The whole life emissions are considered from the landlord's point of view – i.e. excluding the tenant's activities.

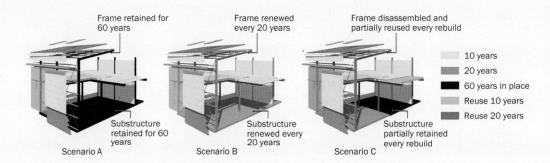

Figure 3.13: Shopping centre scenarios.

Scenario A

This is a baseline option, and assumes continual occupation over the 60-year period. Although this may not be typical for this type of development, it does represent a norm in that it replicates the continuity of a typical high street. A refurbishment cycle has been assumed as follows at year 10 there will be a partial refurbishment and at year 20 a major refurbishment; years 30 and 50 will be as per year 10; years 40 and 60 would be the same as year 20. The structural frame, floor and ground slabs, and roof decking would always be retained.

Scenario B

This represents the more likely life cycle of a typical shopping centre – that is, full redevelopment with all new materials every 20 years (at years 20, 40 and 60). There would be a partial refurbishment or 'refresh' at the intermediate years 10, 30 and 50.

Scenario C

This is the same cycle as scenario B; however, it assumes that the redevelopments at years 20, 40 and 60 include a substantial proportion of onsite recycling of structural members, cladding and other materials. This would include demountable steel frame and assumes reusable concrete plank floor construction. This option also assumes offsite recycling of the unused material.

CARBON EMISSIONS COMPARISON   kg cO$_2$ e/m^2

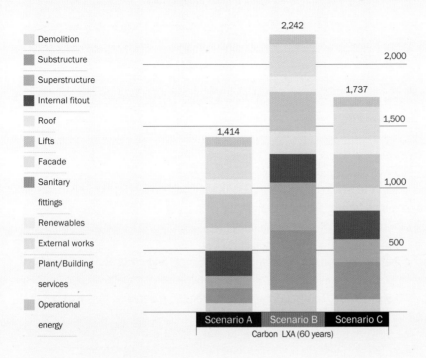

Figure 3.14: Carbon emissions comparison.

Assumptions

- In practice the three scenarios would include many variables. These have been limited, partially for practical reasons and partially to try to isolate the key variables that make the biggest difference. For example, there is no data on the demolition of the previous scheme; however, as we have assumed this would be the same for all three scenarios, it does not make a comparative impact.
- All three scenarios are shown as having the same embodied carbon at practical completion. If you were designing for recycling this would be slightly different in practice – for example, the carbon figures for precast concrete slabs are slightly higher than for in situ slabs.
- In each scenario, it is assumed that the roof finishes, renewables and external works follow the same renewal cycles. They therefore become constants in the comparisons.
- We have also assumed that tenant fitout and churn and associated operational energy use by tenants is a constant between the scenarios.
- The key comparisons are therefore the provision of the shells by the landlord and how the projected life of these shells differs under each scenario in carbon and build cost terms.

Findings

- The overall cheapest in carbon terms is, unsurprisingly, scenario A. However, the difference between scenario A and the full demolition and rebuild in scenario B is 59%, whereas the difference between A and the recycle and rebuild in scenario C is only 23%.
- This clearly shows the carbon benefits of designing for and undertaking wholescale recycling.
- Demolition- and removal-related emissions for B are significantly greater than for A by a factor of nearly 2.5, whereas reuse reduces potential additional carbon emissions by a factor of 1.3.
- The biggest variables are in the substructure. The carbon impacts of rebuilding the substructure every 20 years are huge.
- Superstructure is similar: the whole life carbon quadruples from full retention to continual new build, but only doubles for the recycled option.
- Plant and building services emissions are only slightly greater with the continual new-build option (B) in comparison to the other two scenarios.
- The use of precast concrete slabs is very marginally worse in carbon terms than in situ slabs at practical completion; however, their whole life carbon benefits are apparent in all scenarios over the 60-year period. This is partially due to recycling benefits, and partially due to reduced demolition-related carbon impacts.
- In cost terms over the 60-year period, scenario B is unsurprisingly 54% more expensive than A, whereas the recycling option (C) is 20% cheaper than full replacement (B).

Conclusions

The most carbon-efficient approach is to build a durable building and to keep it, carrying out basic refurbishment as necessary. This suggests that not only the individual buildings should be designed for a long life but also the layout – that is, the 'town planning' – of shopping centres should be designed for the longer term. This implies that the buildings need to be inherently flexible and therefore less prone to commercial redundancy.

Designing for recycling, which implies future flexibility, has clear carbon benefits. It may be too much to expect that a shopping centre will remain unchanged for 60 years but if local adjustments can be achieved easily – ie through flexible construction – then the carbon impacts of such alterations will be less serious. Even if you do not propose to recycle structure on site, designing for easy deconstruction has carbon benefits. Designing for flexible deconstruction aids maintenance and refurbishment.

Wholesale replacement of buildings on a 20-year cycle (or shorter) is very expensive in both carbon and financial terms and very inefficient in terms of resources. Designing for durability, flexibility and a longer life at both the town planning and building scales should help reduce the occurrence of commercial redundancy in this type of shopping centre. Flexible, elemental construction will also help mitigate, in carbon terms, the changes that are likely to occur during a scheme's life.

Low carbon design – macro scale

Overview

Previous chapters have discussed embodied carbon reductions that can be achieved at individual building scale. However, opportunities for further reducing carbon activity are increased when considering large groups of buildings. Whatever the condition or status of the area, campus or district in question, whether it is 'empty' or fully occupied, it is essential to develop a carbon policy or strategy at the outset to specifically inform any master planning or urban regeneration proposals. Experience shows that when the carbon policy is part of the foundation thinking, team engagement is automatic and positive, and carbon reduction is optimised from the outset. For large multi-building development projects, and sites under central ownership or control, such as universities or airports, the carbon policy can be initiated, delivered and controlled centrally. Where central financial control does not exist, for example in a neighbourhood or city, initiating low carbon activity will have a political, administrative or entrepreneurial dimension instead.

Whatever the organisational backdrop, the fundamental issues associated with delivering a low carbon outcome remain the same, even if delivery varies. Large groups of buildings are complex organisms, and delivering low carbon at scale is also complex. However, the whole principle of recycling operates best at scale – the larger the better. The principles of choosing low carbon materials are as discussed elsewhere in this book; however, the best way to maximise the opportunity offered by large clusters of buildings is through deploying the circular economy principle. Recycling should be optimised to the extent that new material is reduced in favour of using recycled material, and new buildings are designed to be capable of beneficial recycling. In any large group of buildings, continuous construction work of one form or another is almost a given. To enable efficient circularity, it is therefore necessary to identify and track all material, and to enable site-wide supply and demand to communicate.

Estate policy and resource planning

Any site-wide low carbon policy should start with assessing what exists across the site, and how it can be most effectively managed. Everything on a site should be seen as a potential carbon asset with a value. It may be possible to realise this value by direct reuse on site; where this is uneconomic, offsite recycling may prove beneficial. As ever, transport is a key consideration in the recycling and reuse equation. Today, existing onsite material is often viewed as redundant trash and therefore a direct project cost. However, with declining resources, such 'trash' will increasingly have a value. Much of this is down to communication: one site's redundant bricks are another site's building material. It is a question of making the commercial connection, followed by the logistical cost – both financial and CO_2e – of delivery. Online building material trading platforms do exist, but are still in their infancy when it comes to providing an efficient contribution to low carbon culture.

Another feature of reuse is that most of today's existing buildings were not originally designed or assembled for future dismantling and reuse. We must evolve a more resource-aware, flexible design approach to buildings post-completion. The ability to reuse an increasing percentage of redundant onsite material will then increase. Large groups of buildings will be able to trade components, and parts of or even whole buildings; large buildings can be reassembled into smaller buildings, and so on. Future low carbon buildings will be made of components that are 100% recyclable, and easy and viable to reuse without significant reprocessing. Waste from consumables will be used to manufacture building materials, and to power the fabrication process. Total flexibility will be fundamental: buildings will be capable of being changed, dismantled, moved and reassembled.

Decisions on existing structures or buildings should start from the premise that they have a carbon value, with the preferred option being that they are retained, reassigned and retrofitted to suit their new role. This should ideally be supported by legislation (tax benefits), town planning (Section 106 rebates, ie credits against the 'planning tax') and BREEAM. Where destruction is unavoidable, the second option is beneficial reuse, which should also be supported by legislation, town planning and BREEAM. Carbon accounting through detailed carbon assessments will enable quantification of such existing structures and their demolition into components. If a building is simple to dismantle and reuse, then it has more value 'as found', even if it is no longer needed. This turns existing redundant buildings from liabilities into assets. Durable, robust buildings also have a significant part to play, provided they are inherently flexible and capable of reuse. Some of the most interesting architectural schemes of the last few decades have been those that include major reuse of, for example, 19th-century building stock. The benefit of this sort of reuse is social and cultural as well as environmental. An example of this is the 2014 Stirling Prize winner, the Everyman Theatre in Liverpool.

A key policy area for consideration in master plan formation is the impact of climate change. Data on this can be conflicting; however, please see the RICS website's dashboard tool,[1] produced by SCP, which enables users to see the impact of climate change on specific non-domestic properties (in the UK, Ireland, France, Germany, Spain, Greece, Norway and Sweden). Futureproofing against climate change helps avoid potential redundancy and waste, and reduces the need for future changes to the fabric (facades in particular) and services.

There is already a huge amount of literature on efficient energy production on large sites and so, consistent with the rest of this book, I will not cover those issues save for the following points. Firstly, for any onsite energy generation, it is essential to look holistically at the carbon costs of installing, maintaining and replacing such systems in comparison to what they produce. Secondly, and related to the first point, it is worth considering energy systems that efficiently feed off waste generated by the site itself. A good example of this is the anaerobic digester, which can deliver electrical power and hot water from food and other organic waste.

Case study 7 looks at delivering low carbon outcomes across a substantial London estate. For Grosvenor, which owns some 5,000 properties in Central London, the issues of achieving holistic low carbon outcomes are as much about determining the appropriate policies and targets as ensuring that their respective project teams, internal project managers, consultants and the supply chain all understand what is required to deliver the optimum outcomes.

Embodied and whole life carbon strategies for campus-type sites

The efficient reuse of materials within a single large estate- or campus-type ownership requires an effective method of collating, ranking and tracking the significant amount of data involved. For estates such as those owned by Grosvenor in London, Gatwick Airport, Argent at King's Cross, or a campus such as Warwick University, geographical information system (GIS) modelling is one of several ways to track such data. GIS modelling is essentially a series of spreadsheets linked to polygons on a plan. The plan can be divided up into individual units, properties, ownerships and so on, which then form the 'cells' of the plan. Each cell is then given attribute data, which can include, for example, EPCs, lease lengths, number of storeys, building age, and material- and carbon-related data. It is then possible to select and compare different site-wide attributes depending on your requirements. It is also possible to divide up the site into a grid, into which attributes can be inserted. GIS makes it possible to create a carbon map of an existing site, giving carbon and material values to existing buildings, infrastructure, etc. As the scheme evolves during design, changes can be tracked as the original carbon map of buildings and materials is supplanted by the proposals over time.

The value to the client may start with carbon mapping but can evolve into a more complex occupier or tenant management tool. For Grosvenor in London, GIS can be used to plan and predict required improvements to EPC performance across the properties within their ownership. This form of centralised planning has clear benefits, but for day-to-day activity a materials tracker with locations and quantities would be much more responsive. This would enable framework contractors and project managers to maximise efficient reuse across the entire estate.

Gatwick Airport is developing a circular economy-inspired embodied carbon strategy that will encourage new buildings to be designed from the outset for possible dismantling, adaptation and reuse. At the simplest level, this would assume a 'kit'-type approach; more practically, the intention is to ensure that new buildings are designed and assembled specifically to facilitate reuse (see case study 8).

CASE STUDY 7:

Grosvenor London estate – carbon strategy

BY SIMON STURGIS

Grosvenor owns some 5,000 properties in Central London, principally in Mayfair and Belgravia. These properties, or the original sites, have been in Grosvenor's ownership for around 300 years and, as it expects to own them for at least another 300 years, it is inclined to take a very long view. This has put Grosvenor at the forefront of sustainable environmental thinking with respect to the properties it controls. This process is anything but static, with Grosvenor undertaking a range of initiatives to improve the environmental performance of this large, urban portfolio. This is known as the 'Living Cities' programme.[2] Within the programme sits general environmental and social performance enhancement through carbon emissions reductions, health and wellbeing, and community engagement.

SCP has been working with Grosvenor from the strategic and policy level through to individual retrofits, and high-performance units (Passivhaus EnerPHit). The overall strategic target for Grosvenor has been to reduce estate-wide operational carbon emissions by 50% over

2013   *2030*

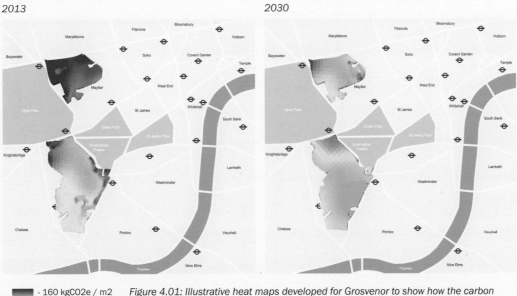

- 160 kgCO2e / m2

- 20 kgCO2e / m2

Figure 4.01: Illustrative heat maps developed for Grosvenor to show how the carbon profile of the estate could change with the sustainable retrofit programme.

the period 2013 to 2023 for directly managed properties. This is currently on target, and is largely achieved through a rolling retrofit and maintenance programme as properties come up for attention each year. While many of the carbon savings may be individually small, over time and across an estate this size the aggregate carbon reduction potential is substantial (approximately 8,500 tCO_2e over 10 years). Each year Grosvenor embarks on further stages of the evolving carbon reduction strategy, such as also tracking and delivering embodied carbon savings.

This is an iterative process with strategic and practical implementation working together. Overall theoretical reduction targets must be based in achievable reality, but should also be sufficiently challenging to move the process forward. These targets include an annual requirement for a number of Passivhaus EnerPHit projects. The lessons learned through these high-performance properties then filter into the general retrofit programme.

The main focus over the last few years has been to optimise the operational emissions performance of Grosvenor's Georgian, Victorian and Edwardian properties, which are invariably listed or in conservation areas. Post completion, a proportion of these properties are closely monitored for environmental performance, including humidity, internal and external temperature, and CO_2. This regime is to establish performance against expectation, relative performance of different strategies (both in CO_2 and monetary terms) and impact on original fabric. This operational-focused strategy is now evolving into a more holistic whole life carbon reduction strategy that includes embodied carbon impacts, targeting cost-neutral and cost-effective measures.

The theory of what needs to be done to achieve embodied and whole life carbon emissions reductions across the London portfolio is understood. Achieving it in practice is another question. The first stage has been to retrospectively analyse a recently completed substantial retrofit project. The following summarises four projects under consideration for evolving and delivering a more comprehensive carbon reduction programme in practice. The aim is to evolve thinking to ensure all stakeholders involved with delivering Grosvenor retrofit projects are fully conversant with low carbon thinking and associated environmental impacts, including the circular economy and future climate change.

Carbon reduction projects

Project 1: Defining embodied carbon reduction targets

A pilot project, 119 Ebury Street, was used as a test case. This completed project had been retrofitted to Grosvenor's highest environmental standards; however, embodied carbon impacts had not been a consideration, although materials had been chosen responsibly. The as-built information was analysed and recommendations were made for a whole range of carbon reduction options. It was possible to identify 23% embodied carbon reductions against what was built. However, following a review by the quantity surveyor 11% were identified as cost-neutral (see Figure 4.03). The implications of this are being tested on three live projects to verify the original findings and develop an estate-wide embodied carbon strategy with targets.

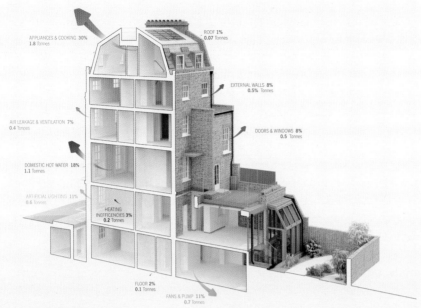

Figure 4.02: 119 Ebury Street.

Carbon footprint
over 60 years

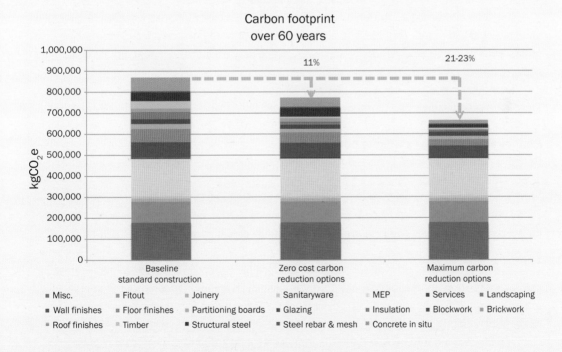

Figure 4.03: 119 Ebury Street – embodied carbon reductions and zero cost.

The following are SCP proposals for research projects to supplement the evolving work already been undertaken by Grosvenor:

Project 2: Purchasing and supply chain review

This research project recognises that, even if the client and design teams are fully on board, the supply chain still needs to be positively managed to achieve decisions taken. It aims to ensure low carbon outcomes from the perspective of low carbon procurement, recycling and the circular economy.

The supply chain across all London projects is examined to see what efficiencies of scale can be identified to achieve low carbon/low cost outcomes. The aim is not to disrupt current procurement activity but to strengthen the hand of contractors in certain key areas to achieve the best low carbon/low cost outcomes, and ensure that any financial benefits of procuring at scale are delivered to Grosvenor.

Project 3: Materials database

There is continual construction activity at varying scales across Grosvenor's London portfolio. Most of this activity involves the disposal of material and the potential for reuse of recycled material. Currently much of this material is taken away by waste contractors who offer '100% recycling'; in reality, this can mean anything other than landfill. The ideal is for items to be recycled at the same level rather than, say, as hardcore for floor slabs.

This project proposes a materials database – a tracker that identifies what is available and links that with need. The aim is to encourage Grosvenor to become a circular economy proponent with a usable inventory of materials, availability and locations that can be used by all construction projects.

To optimise recycling, however, it may be more efficient to connect into a larger pool of recycling materials, eg those run by Salvo[3] or Recipro.[4]

Project 4: Resilience to climate change

By 2050, temperatures are expected to have risen by as much as 2-2.5°C in the summer and 1-1.5°C in the winter.

This translates into additional fuel costs. For example, by 2050 electricity costs for cooling non-domestic buildings are expected to rise by 120% for older buildings, and by 55% for buildings built today. These figures will be partially offset by slightly less expenditure on gas for winter heating.

As a long-term property-holder this is of concern for Grosvenor. The RICS has a climatic risk toolkit for non-domestic real estate;[5] a variation of this could be constructed specifically to understand the impact of climate change across the London Estate, more particularly the residential assets.

The objective would be to ensure the long-term carbon and energy efficiency of the estate and to contribute to reducing overheating, future running costs, carbon emissions and potentially insurance premiums, and improving health and wellbeing, fuel efficiency and future asset value.

CASE STUDY 8:

Gatwick carbon management plan

BY SIMON STURGIS

This case study is of a project commissioned by Gatwick Airport Limited (GAL) in March 2016 to develop an embodied carbon construction policy and plan, with the aim of embedding a circular economy approach to development of the Gatwick estate. GAL already has ambitious reduction targets for Scope 1 and 2 GHG emissions and reports its carbon footprint against GHG Scopes 1, 2 and 3, and in addition against Carbon Trust Standards and Airport Carbon Accreditation (ACA). All of these only cover operational emissions by the airport and third-party users, and not embodied. GAL was keen to begin developing a whole life carbon approach that would enhance overall resource efficiency and introduce circular economic principles into its design and procurement strategies going forward. This would make Gatwick a world leader in carbon management and reporting.

It is important to note that this 'Embodied Carbon Construction Plan' is built environment focused, and does not include transport or aircraft emissions, which are subject to separate initiatives.

A site-wide geographical information system (GIS) carbon management plan was developed that records the carbon and material attributes of all buildings, runways, car parks, taxiways, green areas, etc over the entire estate, above and below ground level. This forms a baseline condition and record of existing fabric against which new projects can be designed and compared. The objective is to ensure a step-change in the carbon footprint over time using low carbon materials, recycled content and circular design principles. In addition, intelligent reuse of building elements and designing for future recycling would produce a downward trajectory for carbon emissions over forthcoming capital expenditure projects. Airports are continually undergoing refurbishment and development, with huge opportunities for low carbon resource management. On to this embodied carbon baseline, future capital investment programmes and also maintenance and operational activities can be tracked from a carbon efficiency perspective.

New capital projects will undergo standard carbon analysis through the RIBA stages. However, the GIS carbon map provides the addition of local project information and the carbon value of existing structure and materials within the project curtilage. The speed at which an airport evolves means that a retrofit project today may within a few years be superseded by a rebuild. The Embodied Carbon Construction Plan enables both forward planning and the ability to review for reuse of any existing materials from across the entire site. New-build projects are also developed within the parameters of the circular economy to ensure that, when the time comes, they can be dismantled and efficiently reused. In aggregate, these activities will enable a more efficient and flexible approach to Gatwick's development portfolio and reduce costs over time. An individual project in this context should be costed not just for delivery at practical completion, but should include life cycle costs as well.

This evolving Embodied Carbon Construction Plan is set in the context of a broader carbon policy. GAL already has sophisticated environmental policies, which continue to evolve. The key feature of GAL's approach to embodied carbon is to ensure joined-up, holistic thinking on all carbon-related activities.

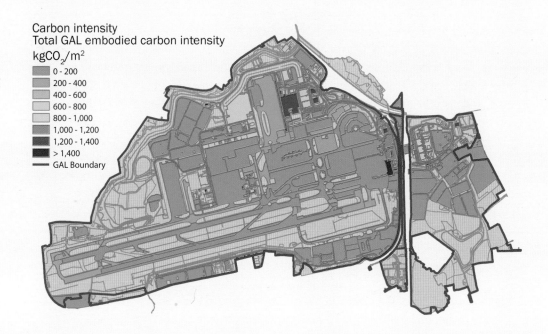

Carbon intensity
Total GAL embodied carbon intensity
$kgCO_2/m^2$

■ 0 - 200
■ 200 - 400
■ 400 - 600
■ 600 - 800
■ 800 - 1,000
■ 1,000 - 1,200
■ 1,200 - 1,400
■ > 1,400
— GAL Boundary

Figure 4.04: Gatwick Airport – embodied carbon intensity.

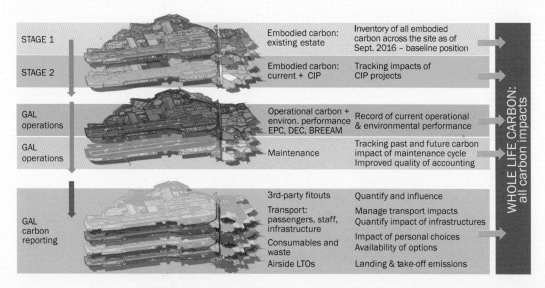

STAGE 1		Embodied carbon: existing estate	Inventory of all embodied carbon across the site as of Sept. 2016 – baseline position
STAGE 2		Embodied carbon: current + CIP	Tracking impacts of CIP projects
GAL operations		Operational carbon + environ. performance EPC, DEC, BREEAM	Record of current operational & environmental performance
GAL operations		Maintenance	Tracking past and future carbon impact of maintenance cycle Improved quality of accounting
GAL carbon reporting		3rd-party fitouts	Quantify and influence
		Transport: passengers, staff, infrastructure	Manage transport impacts Quantify impact of infrastructures
		Consumables and waste	Impact of personal choices Availability of options
		Airside LTOs	Landing & take-off emissions

WHOLE LIFE CARBON: all carbon impacts

Figure 4.05: Gatwick – towards whole life carbon accounting.

Conclusions

Using GIS carbon mapping and applying circular economic principles will make a huge impact on overall airport resource efficiency and consequently carbon emissions reduction. The impact and performance of green areas, such as grass, trees and green roofs, can also be factored into the overall equation. Joined-up thinking across construction, maintenance and the operation of buildings is crucial to avoid the unintended consequences of focusing on one area only. This strategy puts circular economic thinking into practice and at scale, with measureable financial and carbon outcomes.

CASE STUDY 9:

London's airport options

AUTHORS: GARETH ROBERTS AND JUAN J. LAFUENTE

This case study is a reworking of a report prepared for the Airports Commission assessing embodied and whole life carbon impacts of the main options for increasing runway capacity serving London and the south of England.[6]

For simplicity, just two of the options analysed are included. The first is for a new four-runway hub airport in the Thames Estuary, known as the Estuary Airport; the second would build on existing infrastructure to make Gatwick and Stansted two-runway airports with the same potential capacity as Heathrow, and to link them to Central London via faster rail links. The latter is referred to as the Constellation Airports. Both proposals meet the same passenger demand.

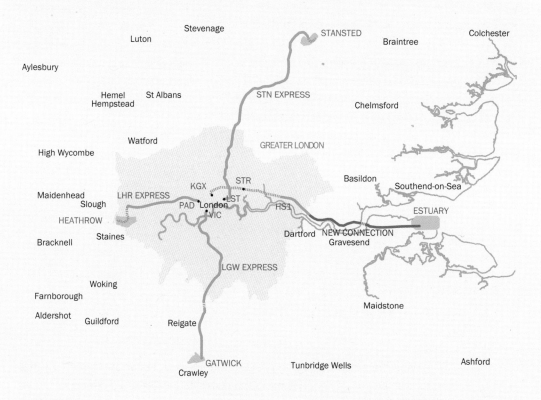

Figure 4.06: Location of current airports around Greater London and proposed new Estuary Airport.

The scope of this evaluation was to assess not only the operational carbon emitted during the airport's everyday activities, but also the embodied carbon required to build, maintain and upgrade the facilities over a 60-year lifespan. Whole life analysis of each scheme is important since the building of the Estuary Airport would require the decommissioning of Heathrow. It should be noted that the scope excluded aircraft movement, specifically taxiing and take-off and landing. The reason for this was the assumption that aircraft movements for the Estuary and the Constellation options (both with a total of six runways) would be effectively the same.

Scope

This includes not just the emissions associated with building the airport itself but also all the emissions from associated structures and infrastructure that support it. The emissions sources are classified as follows:

Construction, upgrade, and use of the airport facilities such as terminals, runways, hangars, etc. Depending on the location, the airport construction may include large amounts of reclaimed land. The carbon emitted in the process of demolishing any airport was included.

Construction of facilities directly associated with airport activities but often located outside their limits, such as warehouses, hotels and car parks. The quantity of these facilities is dependent on the type of services an airport offers, as well as the routes and passengers they serve.

The construction and upgrade of transport infrastructure such as railway lines, train stations or highways to access the airports.

Passengers accessing the airport. These emissions vary depending on factors like travel distance, accessibility to different modes of transport and passengers' preferences.

The two proposals

As per the Department for Transport's latest forecasts (2013), both proposals meet the capacity of 210 million passengers per year.[7] The key characteristics of each scheme are:

Estuary Airport

- New four-runway airport hub built in the Thames Estuary
- Half of the airport footprint is built on land reclaimed from the sea
- Heathrow Airport would close and be demolished
- Gatwick and Stansted airports would operate with one runway each

Constellation Airports

- Uses the embodied carbon assets already built in current infrastructures
- One new runway each is added to Gatwick and Stansted airports
- Heathrow Airport operates at current capacity
- Three similar sized airports around Greater London

Estuary Airport

This proposal is for a four-runway airport located in the Thames Estuary with capacity for 142 million passengers. The additional 68 million would be provided for by Gatwick and Stansted, which would operate with one runway each. Heathrow would be closed and demolished.

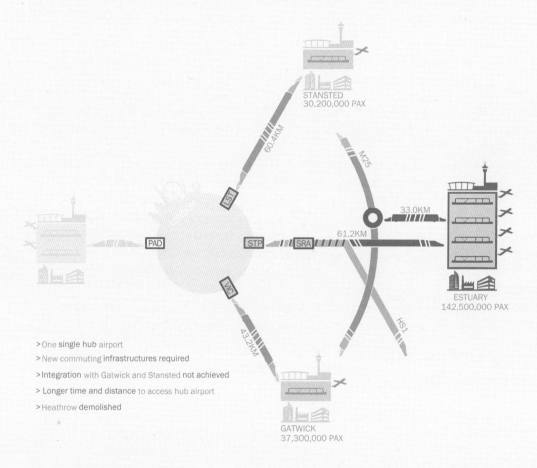

Figure 4.07: Estuary Airport scenario.

Benefits
*   **Single major international hub airport:** It might be the only practical answer to avoid patching solutions.
*   **Acoustic pollution:** A well-located and planned hub will diminish the nuisance to population.
*   **Transfer airport:** It will provide more connecting possibilities to passengers whose final destination is not London.

Disadvantages
*   **Location:** Over 60km away from London, further than any airport currently operating.
*   **Market:** Since London is the final destination for 78% of passengers, it is not certain that a hub is required.
*   **Heathrow would need to close:** This would entail a massive relocation of companies, infrastructures and people – some figures predict that up to 75,000 jobs would need to move.
*   **Accessibility:** A single airport may be conveniently located for Central London and some nearby regions but it will be difficult to access for the majority of the UK population.
*   **Major investment in new infrastructures:** New infrastructures will be required to connect a currently unpopulated area with no infrastructures.
*   **Flexibility issues:** Phasing of additional capacity is difficult to implement for a hub airport.

Constellation Airports

The second proposal adds one runway at Stansted and another at Gatwick, creating a constellation of three main airports of similar size around London. Heathrow would operate at a slightly higher capacity after upgrade plans to improve efficiency.

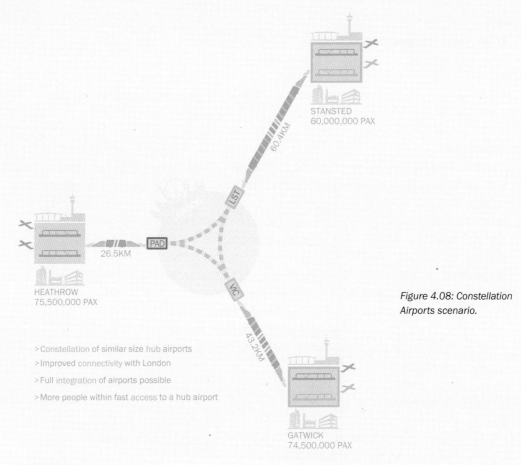

STANSTED
60,000,000 PAX

60.4KM

LST

PAD   26.5KM

HEATHROW
75,500,000 PAX

VIC

43.2KM

> Constellation of similar size hub airports
> Improved connectivity with London
> Full integration of airports possible
> More people within fast access to a hub airport

GATWICK
74,500,000 PAX

Figure 4.08: Constellation Airports scenario.

Benefits

- **Existing facilities:** Upgrading existing infrastructures will require less investment – and **fewer** carbon emissions.
- **Location:** All airports are closer to London's city centre and give **more** choice to the rest of the UK population.
- **Accessibility – UK:** Shorter travel distance and direct connection to at least **one** major airport will provide most UK regions with a wider range of transport **modes** to choose from.
- **Accessibility – London:** The airports **are already connected** to Central London **via existing rail lines; upgrading these** will be simpler than creating new links.
- **Flexible delivery:** Airports expansion can be phased.

Disadvantages

- **Older infrastructures:** Updated infrastructure may not work as efficiently as new.
- **Acoustic pollution:** The **number** of people subject to noise pollution will not decrease.
- **No major hub:** Does not give the UK the potential to become a major European airport hub.

Building the airports – embodied carbon emissions

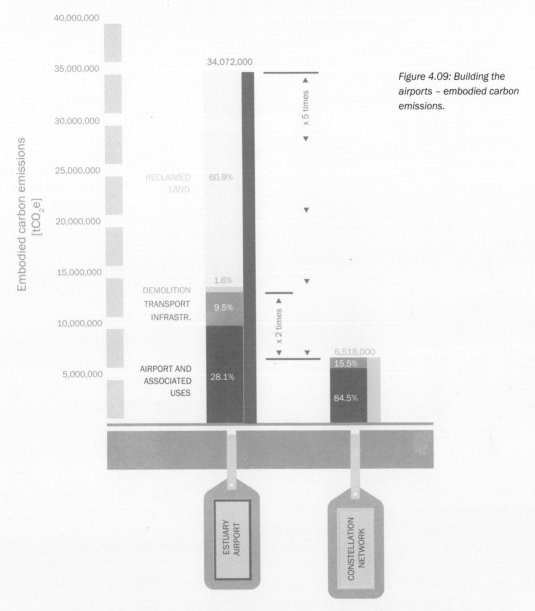

Figure 4.09: Building the airports – embodied carbon emissions.

- The construction of the new Estuary Airport would emit 34 million tonnes of CO_2e –more than five times more CO_2e than building the Constellation Airports.
- 34 million tonnes of CO_2e is more than the annual carbon emissions of New Zealand.
- The construction of the new airport facilities and their associated uses in the Estuary Airport would emit 70% more CO_2e (4.2 million tonnes) than completing the existing facilities in the Constellation Airports.
- 4.2 million tonnes of CO_2e is the equivalent of building more than 50,000 new homes.

Travelling to the airport – route operational carbon emissions

Variable operational carbon emissions depend on the airport location. They include commuting to and from the airport and have been estimated using Civil Aviation Authority (CAA) passenger survey statistics.[8]

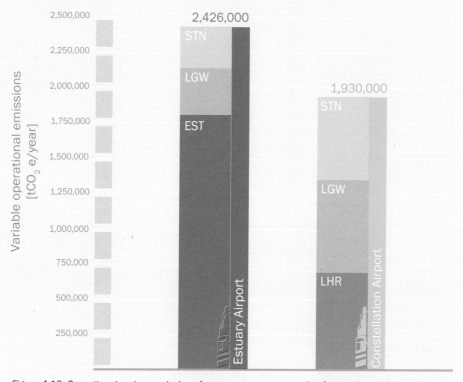

Figure 4.10: Operational carbon emissions from passengers accessing future airports in London.

- The Estuary Airport would emit 500,000 tonnes of CO_2e more per year than the Constellation Airports – 25% more annual emissions.
- Over 30 years, the Estuary Airport would therefore emit 33% more CO_2e than the Constellation Airports.
- Over 60 years, the difference between the CO_2e emissions accrued by going to and from the Estuary Airport would be double that of the Constellation Airports.

Whole life carbon impact

Over 35 years (after which time the CAA predicts further airport capacity will be needed), the Estuary Airport will have emitted 63% (43m tonnes CO_2e) more than the Constellation Airports option for the same capacity and demand.

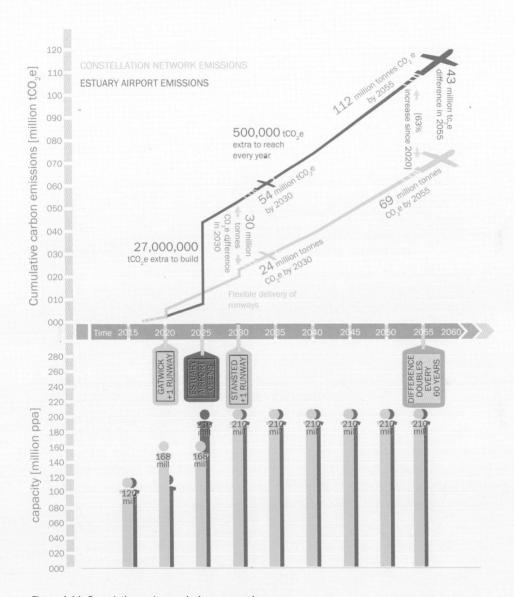

Carbon impacts of Estuary and
Constellation Network oroposals
[embodied and variable operational emissions only]

Figure 4.11: Cumulative carbon emissions comparison.

This study shows that the embodied carbon emissions impacts at the scale of major
infrastructure projects is vast compared to individual buildings, and should be central to the
consideration of such projects. Opportunities exist for the reduction of these impacts and need
to be addressed. The next case study takes a wider look at transport infrastructure.

CASE STUDY 10:

Transport infrastructure

BY GARETH ROBERTS AND JUAN J. LAFUENTE

This study evolved from case study 9 to look at the broader issue of transport infrastructure and carbon.

A quarter of the UK's carbon emissions arise from transport. Although evaluating infrastructure is complex, there is huge potential for this sector to help the UK to meet its target of reducing carbon emissions by 80% by 2050.

This case study gives a glimpse into the world of carbon footprinting for large UK infrastructure projects. It illustrates how such appraisals differ from previous building-based carbon assessment studies by including the passenger and travel distance.

To illustrate these issues is an excerpt from SCP's 2013 report for the independent Airports Commission on the future of London's airports. The report shows that if carbon emissions (meaning the whole bundle of greenhouse gases and carbon dioxide equivalents, including methane, nitrous oxide and CFCs) had been made a deciding factor in the location of London's new airport, it could have saved the equivalent of 3.5% of the UK's annual greenhouse gas emissions over a seven-year period.

So how does the carbon footprinting of infrastructure projects compare to that of individual buildings? The main difference arises not from the aggregation methods and data but from the techniques employed to understand the findings. Transport is all about moving people, so it is not just a question of amounts per unit of area but more about how efficiently we move someone from A to B – that is, the carbon impact per person per kilometre. For most transport types, it is likely that the construction of an interchange or station generates large amounts of carbon emissions, which should also be included in any appraisal.

By way of illustration, travelling by boat generates very little carbon emissions in movement, but the construction of harbours (and ships) is responsible for enormous amounts of embodied carbon. Compare this with, say, travelling by car, which generates up to nine times more carbon emissions per passenger per km but has a smaller initial embodied carbon investment, generally limited to the vehicle itself and its share of the road infrastructure. This is not to give the impression that travel by car is always best for short distances and travel by boat best for long – it is more complicated than that. However, the main issues can be summarised under the following four headings:

Fixed and variable embodied carbon emissions
Building a terminal produces a 'fixed' amount of carbon, but the emissions associated with the construction of routes (roads, railways, etc) vary depending on distance. Understanding this point is important when dealing with modes of transport that require large embodied carbon expenditures to create terminal facilities.

Relationship between embodied and operational carbon per mode of transport
Understanding this is important to ensure that we are not swayed by modes of transport (such as shipping) that have low operational movement costs but enormous hidden embodied costs at the port facilities themselves. The same logic applies to rail and, in particular, large tunnelling projects such as the Channel Tunnel or the Gotthard Tunnel under the Swiss Alps.

Accessibility and catchment areas
Large infrastructures such as airports and terminal stations are destinations in themselves. It is therefore important to understand the carbon impacts generated by passengers getting to and from the station or airport, and not just the impacts of the onward journeys.

System thinking
In reality, people's choices are dynamic. Car drivers may become train passengers if a faster train line is built into a city, but they may revert to driving if fares are increased too much. Understanding this point is important in evaluating proposals where more than one type of infrastructure is being provided, as composite effects may accrue.

Figure 4.12 illustrates how different modes of transport compare in terms of embodied and operational carbon emissions. It also identifies whether the emissions are generated by the construction/use of the terminal or the route. Figures are presented per person per km over a 60-year life cycle and the predicted passenger capacity over this timeframe. The interrelations of these sources define the character and possibilities of each mode of transport.

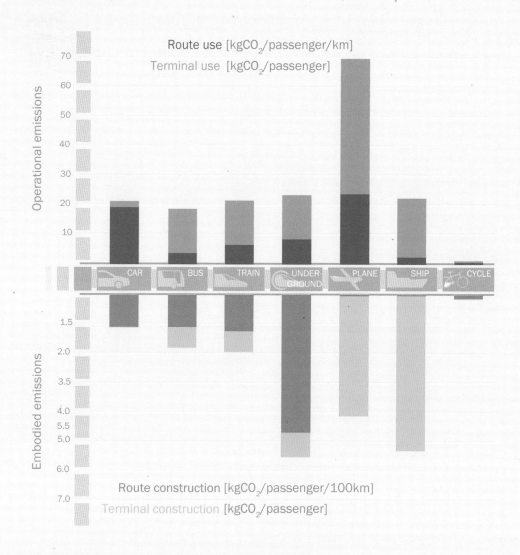

Figure 4.12: Embodied and operational carbon for different modes of transport.

The graph confirms some basic intuitive trends: investing in large terminal facilities is only worthwhile from a carbon perspective when the onward transport route costs are low and long distances are to be travelled. Similarly, investing in public infrastructure with high embodied route costs is only worthwhile if the cars are displaced from congested roads.

Figure 4.13 shows a simplified view of the transport world where all fixed terminal and variable route costs are taken into consideration. Please note that this graph is not intended to provide a basis for individuals to choose means of transport but more for transport planners considering aggregate choices for a whole population. For instance, if the average journey distance on a railway between two stations was shorter than 100km and uncongested travel by car on a motorway was an alternative, investing in the road infrastructure would be the better solution from a carbon perspective since the rail link's whole life carbon costs would be greater. If, on the other hand, the rail terminal on this route can be shared with other, longer distance routes, travel by rail becomes vastly more attractive.

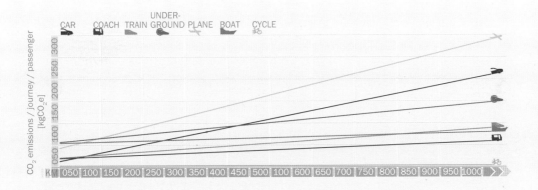

Figure 4.13: Relationship between emissions generated by the construction of terminal facilities and those generated on route.

The initial construction of a Central London underground station generates more embodied carbon on a per passenger basis over a 60-year lifespan (including maintenance and repair) than any other infrastructure types analysed. Travelling by bike is by far the best from an operational and embodied perspective – however, the embodied carbon of the cyclist's additional food consumption was not included in this analysis!

Conclusions

1. **Embodied carbon emissions: different impacts of terminals and routes**
   The 'fixed' carbon costs to build terminals differ greatly from the variable carbon costs for routes. Distance becomes a critical factor to be considered: airport construction has a high terminal carbon impact. Decisions on where to build an airport should be based on catchment areas of air passengers accessing the airport, because emissions generated by passengers getting to the airport are by far the most significant factor influencing carbon emissions over its lifetime.

2. **Relative impacts between embodied and operational emissions**
   Modes of transport with high terminal construction embodied costs are more suitable for long distance routes with low operational costs. This is well illustrated by boat travel – the embodied carbon emissions of building the terminal (harbour) are some of the highest while the operational emissions of travel are some of the lowest. The crucial point here is not to be swayed by operational impacts alone.

3. **Commuting to terminals**
   Major terminal buildings are destinations in themselves. Reducing distances to terminals by locating them in catchment areas with high numbers of users is critical to reducing the embodied and also the operational carbon emissions. Distribution of population and accessibility to different modes of transport are also essential parts of the equation to be considered: sometimes locating a major terminal further away from a major city will emit less carbon if the catchment area for interregional commuting is larger.

4. **System thinking**
   Where more than one mode of transport is available, people's dynamic choices should be considered. Factors like ticket fares or ease of transfer between modes of transport when carrying luggage might drive people choices towards longer, less convenient or more highly emitting possibilities.

5

Low carbon design – human scale

Carbon emissions can be reduced at all scales, and changes to individual behaviour can make a significant difference. For example, in the book *How Bad are Bananas?*, Mike Berners-Lee shows that switching from a cappuccino at $235gCO_2e$ to a black coffee at $21gCO_2e$ represents a +90% improvement.[1] Individually this is a small saving, but by changing the coffee habits of a nation the savings are potentially huge. The aim of this chapter is to view the somewhat abstract notion of carbon emissions in the built environment on a more understandable and human scale.

The EU has noted that, since conventional emissions reduction strategies are unlikely to deliver the targeted reductions (80% reductaion from 1990 levels by 2050), behavioural change needs to be examined in much greater detail. This will require a significant cultural shift in our understanding of our individual impacts on climate change, and the overall resource efficiency of our behaviour.

As individuals, we tend to feel that our contribution to carbon emissions reduction would be negligible. The city of Marseille showed how this can be overcome. Marseille was notorious for having a terrible and seemingly unsolvable problem with public space rubbish. A private citizen devised the '1 Déchet par Jour' (one piece of rubbish per day) strategy, which encouraged all citizens to pick up and dispose of one item of rubbish every day and record it on social media. In only a few months, Marseilles was transformed. What we need is a similar 'cultural kicker' that moves us towards a more comprehensive awareness of how to live a lower carbon lifestyle. We need to achieve cultural changes in response to climate change, and to realise that the resource efficiency and choices of every one of us matter. We live in a phenomenally profligate society where our current levels of consumption and disposal are just not sustainable. Whether it's avoiding milk in your coffee or keeping your iPhone for an extra two years, it all counts.

Case studies 12 and 13 look at the impacts of individuals' activities and the consequent emissions and puts them into the context of building emissions. Case study 13 owes particular thanks and apologies to Mike Berners-Lee and his book.

CASE STUDY 11:

King's Cross – individual carbon footprinting

BY GARETH ROBERTS AND MAIIA WILLIAMS

This case study is based on an occupier survey undertaken for Argent LLP across its development site at King's Cross, London. The objective was to understand the individual carbon footprints of a representative sample of site users. The client wanted to understand the scale of individual carbon emissions in relation to other site-generated emissions, such as operational, embodied, transport, etc. Work was already being done on individual buildings and internal fitouts but it seemed likely that there were significant areas of emissions that were not being covered.

We were required to understand the make-up of the carbon footprint of King's Cross occupiers of different types, how that compared to the average Londoner, and how it could be reduced. This would lead to a series of recommendations and actions that would enable practical personal reductions. We started with an in-depth occupier survey of a cross-section of site users and discovered that there was potential for significant carbon reductions from relatively small behaviour changes. The following is a summary of what was produced.

The King's Cross development is considered an exemplary working environment. Every office building within the development integrates the latest technology and targets significant reductions in energy consumption and running costs. The site is also considered to be one of the best connected areas in London. The average office occupier contributes 37% less carbon during their commute than a typical Londoner.

Nonetheless, the average King's Cross occupier is 2,050kgCO_2e/annum more carbon-intensive than the average Londoner. The differences in their lifestyle choices (possibly wealth-driven) are identified in Figure 5.01. Combined, this is represents a total potential saving of 98,400tCO_2e/annum. This is a significant CO_2 saving, and is equivalent to constructing a building of some 9,000m² every year.

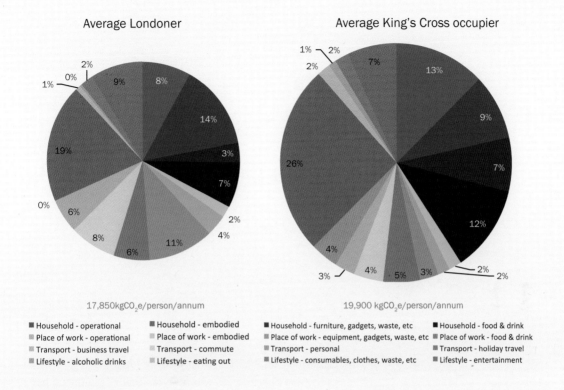

Average Londoner

8%
14%
3%
7%
2%
4%
11%
6%
8%
0%
6%
19%
1%
0%
2%
9%

17,850kgCO$_2$e/person/annum

Average King's Cross occupier

7%
13%
9%
7%
12%
2%
2%
3%
5%
4%
3%
4%
26%
2%
2%
1%
1%
2%

19,900 kgCO$_2$e/person/annum

■ Household - operational   ■ Household - embodied   ■ Household - furniture, gadgets, waste, etc   ■ Household - food & drink
■ Place of work - operational   ■ Place of work - embodied   ■ Place of work - equipment, gadgets, waste, etc ■ Place of work - food & drink
■ Transport - business travel   ■ Transport - commute   ■ Transport - personal   ■ Transport - holiday travel
■ Lifestyle - alcoholic drinks   ■ Lifestyle - eating out   ■ Lifestyle - consumables, clothes, waste, etc   ■ Lifestyle - entertainment

Figure 5.01: Breakdown of CO$_2$e emissions for the average Londoner v average King's Cross occupier.

To simplify the results, the comparable occupier typologies were grouped into two categories: workplace (office workers, retail workers and university students) and residential (private and social housing). Focusing on site-related emissions, a significant difference was identified between these two typologies, with residential being the bigger contributor.

More specifically, 23% of the total CO$_2$e emissions of the typical King's Cross workplace occupier are associated with the site, including building energy consumption, daily commute, lunch, hot drinks, printing, workplace waste, etc. People who live in King's Cross spend more than 50% of their total CO$_2$e emissions on site, including household energy consumption as well as gadgets, home appliances, weekly food shopping, local gym visits and other lifestyle choices.

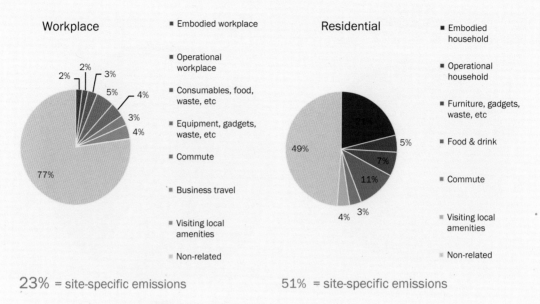

Figure 5.02: Site-specific CO$_2$e emissions for King's Cross; workspace occupiers v residential occupiers.

Alternatively, to show the actual site-specific carbon impacts, an indicative footprint for workplace and residential occupiers is shown in Figure 5.03, where the output is expressed per person per year.

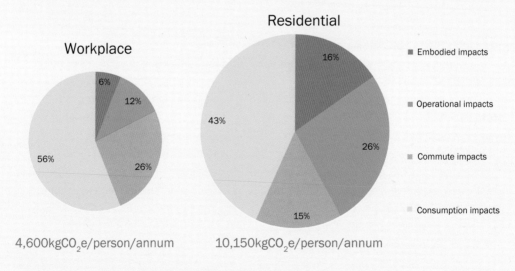

Figure 5.03: An indicative split of the carbon impacts associated with the King's Cross site. (For total emissions, refer to figure 5.02.)

To put things in perspective, the average Londoner's overall footprint is double that of a homeless person in the UK, which in turn is double the impact of the global average. Given the numbers, it seemed probable that improvement in personal carbon footprinting would be achievable at King's Cross.

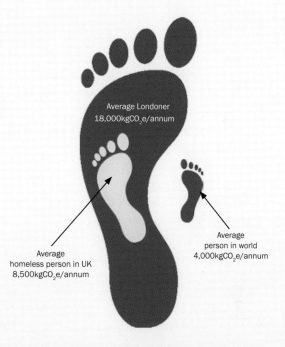

Figure 5.04: The average Londoner's footprint.

Average Londoner
18,000kgCO$_2$e/annum

Average homeless person in UK
8,500kgCO$_2$e/annum

Average person in world
4,000kgCO$_2$e/annum

Overview

Overall, the occupants responsible for the majority of the site-related carbon footprint are private and affordable housing occupiers, followed by office workers and students, with students having the smallest impact (around five times less than private housing occupiers). This uneven distribution of site-related carbon was expected due to the high embodied carbon footprint of households and low operational and embodied carbon footprint of workplaces. In fact, the embodied carbon of households is seven times larger than the equivalent for a place of work. Furthermore, the uneven income of students, and office and retail workers also affects lifestyle choices, resulting in higher footprints for the higher earners.

Key statistics for King's Cross occupiers

Some statistics relating to the habits of King's Cross occupiers were identified from the questionnaires and are summarised below:

- The largest personal footprint was 33,911kgCO$_2$e – almost double the London average
- The smallest personal footprint was 6,026kgCO$_2$e – 66% lower than the London average
- 58% of office workers surveyed cycle or walk to work
- There are, on average, 7.25km between an occupier's household and office/university
- No (or no awareness of) renewables in any household
- 38% of King's Cross occupiers own or share a car
- No smart meter installed in any household
- Three people per household on average
- Two annual holiday flights per person on average
- 58% of participants are meat-eaters

Summary

The estimated eventual occupiers of the King's Cross site will be divided into: 35,000 office workers, 5,000 staff and students, 8,000 residents. Therefore, if all the occupiers implement the savings suggested below, the King's Cross site can benefit from a potential reduction of approximately 98,400tCO_2e/annum.

The following recommendations are a guide to reducing individual carbon footprints. Not all the options will be feasible for every person; nonetheless, they represent the maximum opportunity to reduce carbon footprint.

- **Do not drive (for distances under 3.25km).** If you own a car, not driving short distances can save 1,700kgCO_2e/annum, or £175 of diesel per year.
- **Improve thermal performance of your house.** Installation of insulation and better glazing can save up to 1,200kgCO_2e/annum, or £245 per year.
- **Switch to better boiler.** Operational energy savings of approximately 1,000kgCO_2e/annum, or £200 per year.
- **Install 3kW of PVs in your home.** 9m² of PV panels will halve your electricity bill and save you around 900kgCO_2e/annum and up to £560 per year.
- **Install solar thermal panels in your home.** By installing two panels, you can save around £100 per year and reduce your carbon emissions by 550kgCO_2e/annum.
- **Bring packed lunch to work.** It will save you money and carbon (approximately 550kgCO_2e/annum).
- **Use A++ rated appliances and avoid tumble drying.** It will reduce your energy bill by £230 a year (450kgCO_2e/annum).
- **Use Eurostar instead of flying to Europe once a year.** This saves 90% of CO_2 per journey (381kgCO_2e/annum).
- **Choose to eat vegetarian dishes more often.** Not eating beef or pork 50% of the time will cut 350kgCO_2e/annum.
- **One less latte a day** – or not having milk with your tea – will save 124kgCO_2e/annum.
- **Install a smart meter in your home.** Contact your energy provider – it can save you £20 a year, or 120kgCO_2e/annum.
- **Recycle more.** Simply making sure paper ends up in the right bin could save 110kgCO_2e/annum.
- **One less trip to the pub a month.** Drinking two fewer alcoholic beverages a month can save you £120, or 104kgCO_2e/annum.

The next case study looks at a single consumable – a cup of coffee – and puts such lifestyle choices in the context of those associated with buildings on a per person basis.

CASE STUDY 12:

The impact of lifestyle choices

BY JUAN J LAFUENTE

We make lifestyle choices every day – from the coffee we prefer every morning to the new gadget we want to buy – and most of them have a very small carbon impact as single actions. However, the cumulative effect of everyday habits can generate a greater environmental impact than the homes and offices we occupy.[2]

Figure 5.05 shows the carbon impact of an average Londoner's lifestyle choices. 72% of his or her carbon emissions come from lifestyle choices, as opposed to 28% from buildings. In fact, the carbon emissions from the average Londoner's holiday travel is very similar to the carbon impact of their home.

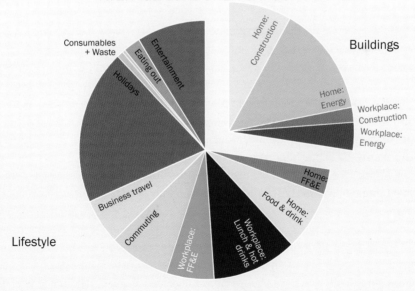

Figure 5.05: The average Londoner's carbon profile.

The global impact of the carbon emissions generated by Londoners is not small. Annual carbon emissions have reached 17,850kgCO_2e per Londoner, making them 4.5 times more carbon intensive than the average person on the planet. 8.5 million Londoners would require a forest as large as the UK and Ireland combined to balance the environmental damage that they cause each year.

The carbon footprint of your coffee

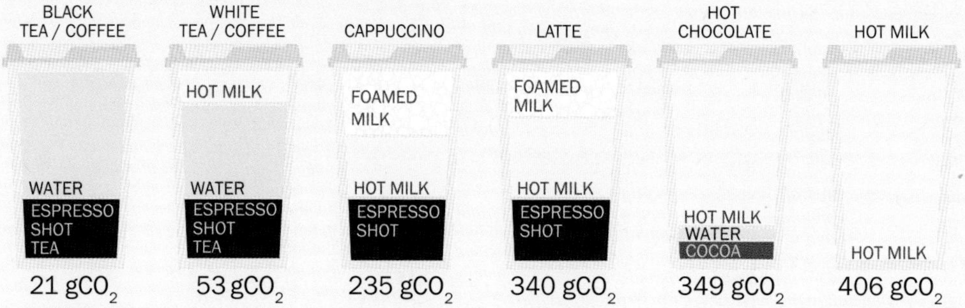

BLACK TEA / COFFEE	WHITE TEA / COFFEE	CAPPUCCINO	LATTE	HOT CHOCOLATE	HOT MILK
	HOT MILK	FOAMED MILK	FOAMED MILK		
WATER ESPRESSO SHOT TEA	WATER ESPRESSO SHOT TEA	HOT MILK ESPRESSO SHOT	HOT MILK ESPRESSO SHOT	HOT MILK WATER COCOA	HOT MILK
21 gCO_2	53 gCO_2	235 gCO_2	340 gCO_2	349 gCO_2	406 gCO_2

Figure 5.06: Whole-Life Carbon impact of different hot drinks

Producing the average latte creates 16 times more carbon emissions than a black coffee.[3] The ingredient responsible for this huge difference is milk. You might have thought that the highest impact for hot drinks would be transportation, since cocoa, tea and coffee are not locally sourced in the UK. However, products with such long lives are normally shipped – one of the least emitting means of transport. Milk, on the other hand, comes from one of the least carbon friendly livestock. Cows are big animals and feeding them to adult stage emits a large amount of carbon. They are also ruminants (ie they chew cud) and their digestive system emits large quantities of methane to the atmosphere, doubling the carbon footprint of milk. The more milk your drink contains, the higher your carbon emissions.

Frequency amplifies the impact of lifestyle choices and their carbon saving potential. The carbon difference between hot drinks options is relatively big, but the emissions of any of them compared with other sectors – like construction or cooling loads – are tiny. However, the long-term impact of changing your habits tells a completely different story. How many coffees do you have every day at work? Two? That adds up to ten coffees a week on average, or around 500 coffees a year. How many years do you need to work before you reach your well-deserved retirement day? Let's assume 35 years – or 17,500 coffees. If you had switched your latte for a white coffee when you started your career, you could have saved around 5,000kg of CO_2e by your retirement day, which is the same amount of carbon that your work laptop will have emitted over the same period.

Five actions to reduce your carbon footprint by 10%

1. Homemade Meat Free Mondays lunch meatfreemondays.com

Meat Free Mondays is a fun and easy international initiative that can generate a relatively large impact. It also encourages lunch options that won't need reheating at work, saving even more carbon. You could try engaging a group of co-workers in the initiative, or even promoting the routine through the whole workplace. If successful, you could aim to add another day in the second year, as long as the drop-out risk is low. The aim is to feel healthier and fitter and save carbon on the way.

By engaging in Meat Free Mondays over 20 years, you could compensate for the carbon emitted in the manufacture of 5,300 bricks (enough bricks to build all the walls in a two-bedroom flat).

2. Go sober for October gosober.org.uk

This one isn't easy at first but it gets better once you figure out what to order in your local pub – and it's also limited to a set timeframe. Reclaiming your Sunday mornings and even donating the money saved to a charity are extra incentives.

Your first sober October will compensate for the carbon emitted by your work laptop for the entire next year.

3. Cycle to work three days a week cyclescheme.co.uk

Hopping on a bike for your commute has a huge carbon saving potential and, of course, countless other benefits: you will feel much healthier and fitter; you can forget about traffic jams, waiting for buses, packed carriages and fuel prices; and you will also be able to predict how long your commute will take. The government's cycle-to-work scheme also allows you to enjoy a brand-new bike with a generous tax deduction.

If you cycle to work three days a week, you will compensate for the carbon emitted annually by the lighting consumption of a two-bedroom flat.

4. Take a train instead of a plane for your next trip to Europe

Flying is by far the most polluting means of transport. A single long-haul flight can triple your personal annual holiday emissions. Frequent flights will vastly multiply emissions: a UK company that needs to fly to New York once a month will have easily emitted in 30 years as much carbon as was used to construct the building they are based in. In such cases, video conferences are recommended. For closer destinations, the European high-speed rail network makes many Continental cities easily accessible.

One return flight to Paris accounts for 2% of the average Londoner's annual carbon emissions. One return flight to New York accounts for 16%.

5. Ditch screens in the evenings

Most of us spend a lot of time in the evenings watching TV series, or on social media, but we may also wish we were using that time more productively. The key to successfully implementing this strategy is to find suitable, less carbon-intensive activities that are also personal and rewarding. Did you play a musical instrument when you were younger? Try playing again for around three evenings a week. Were you an avid reader of comics and graphic novels? Maybe you should visit the loft and retrieve your old collection. Learn French, play board games with your kids, socialise with your flatmates – the options are countless. Find the one that suits you best.

If the average household stopped using mobile phones and computers in the evenings, up to 20% of their heating carbon emissions could be compensated.

Methodology

This book is intended as a guide to carbon emissions and the built environment rather than a precise technical textbook. Therefore, this chapter is an introduction to the current state of embodied and whole life carbon methodology. It is worth noting that progress in this area is speeding up through both the IWLCIB/RICS project (due 2017) mentioned in the Introduction, and BREEAM 2018, which together are expected to bring WLC into the mainstream.

The principal measurement metrics described in this chapter for assessing whole life carbon efficiency are BS EN 15978[1] (and 15804 materials),[2] life cycle analysis (LCA), marginal abatement cost curve analysis (MAC curves) and carbon cost analysis (CCA). Together, these provide for comprehensive assessment of whole life carbon emissions and the economic costs and benefits of the low carbon options under consideration, and the ability to understand and measure reuse, recycling and the circular economy.

Background

Carbon emissions reporting sits within greenhouse gas (GHG) emissions reporting, as described in the UK government's July 2009 Low Carbon Transition Plan[3] and the Low Carbon Industrial Strategy.[4] The extract below, on scopes 1, 2 and 3 emissions, is from 'Guidance on how to measure and report your greenhouse gas emissions':

Scope 1 (Direct emissions)
Activities owned or controlled by your organisation that release emissions straight into the atmosphere. They are direct emissions. Examples of scope 1 emissions include emissions from combustion in owned or controlled boilers, furnaces, vehicles; emissions from chemical production in owned or controlled process equipment.

Scope 2 (Energy indirect)
Emissions being released into the atmosphere associated with your consumption of purchased electricity, heat, steam and cooling. These are indirect emissions that are a consequence of your organisation's activities but which occur at sources you do not own or control.

Scope 3 (Other indirect)

Emissions that are a consequence of your actions, which occur at sources which you do not own or control and which are not classed as scope 2 emissions. Examples of scope 3 emissions are business travel by means not owned or controlled by your organisation, waste disposal, or purchased materials or fuels.[5]

Embodied carbon emissions as described in this book sit within scope 3, in that the materials that we use are produced by others and would be counted as their scope 1 or 2 emissions. Whole life carbon, in relation to a building, falls under scopes 1, 2 and 3 emissions.

Implementing the British Standard BS EN 15978

(Refer to RICS Professional Statement: Whole Life carbon measurement: Implementation in the built environment 2017' for detailed definitions)

In November 2011, the British Standard BS EN 15978:2011 was published,[6] deriving from the European CEN/TC 350 standard[7] and bringing it into the British Standards framework. As shown in the summarising diagram below, BS EN 15978 sets out a whole life methodology, covering operational carbon emissions, from both energy and water use (B6 & B7), and embodied emissions (A1-A5, B1-B5, C1-C4 and D). This is the basis on which embodied and whole life carbon emissions are understood and assessed today.

BS EN 15978 covers entire buildings, while the associated BS EN 15804 covers materials. Ideally these two Standards should be read together. Other relevant Standards are PAS 2050,[8] PAS 2080[9] and the ISO 14000 series.[10]

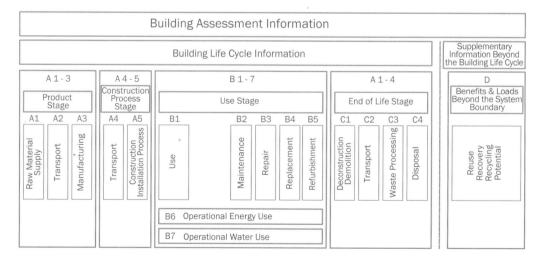

Figure 6.01: BS EN 15978:2011 – display of modular information for the different stages of the building assessment.

The following explains the practical aspects and scopes of delivering a whole life carbon assessment on a project. This summary goes beyond the British Standard to answer some of the specific questions that arise from undertaking such an assessment in practice.

Boundaries

The assessment should cover all works relating to the proposed building and its intended use, including its foundations, external works within the site, and all adjacent land associated with its typical operations. A planning 'red line' can serve as the boundary if applicable. As a minimum, an assessment should be undertaken both at design stage, ie 'as designed', and post practical completion, ie 'as built'. Ideally an assessment should also be undertaken at tender stage to identify design stage carbon reductions and provide an up-to-date 'carbon budget' for the main contractor. Further localised assessments can be made to examine, for example, structural or cladding options during the design stages.

Physical characteristics

All items within the project's cost plan/bill of quantities should be assessed. This would include the building components listed in table 6.01 on page 102.

Reasonable assumptions should be made for provisional sums, and the assessment should cover at least 90% of the cost of each building element category to accommodate the cost efficiency of the assessment.

Reference study period

For all building types an assessment should be 60 years although for shorter life expectancies the anticipated life expectancy can be used. For Infrastructure the period should be 100 years, although for shorter life expectancies the anticipated life expectancy can be used.

Life cycle stages

The WLC assessment should consider all emissions produced over the entire life of the building per the above periods (cradle to grave). Resource efficiency and carbon footprint optimisation also require taking into account future reusability/recyclability of the different elements that make up the building (cradle to cradle). Therefore, all life cycle stages defined by BS EN 15978 (A1-A5, B1-B7, C1-C4, D) should be included in WLC studies.

Floor area measurement

This should be in accordance with Royal Institute of Chartered Surveyors (RICS) property measurement standards (2015 onwards).[11] The recommended floor areas sources are listed in order of preference: 1) cost plan/bill of quantities; 2) schedule of accommodation/architectural drawings; 3) BIM model; 4) other.

0 Facilitating works	0.1 Hazardous materials treatment and removal	
	0.2 Demolition works	
	0.3 Temporary/enabling works	
	0.4 Specialist groundworks	
1 Substructure	1.1 Foundations incl. excavations	
	1.2 Basement retaining walls	
	1.3 Lowest floor slab	
2 Superstructure	2.1 Frame	
	2.2 Upper floors incl. balconies	
	2.3 Roof	
	2.4 Stairs and ramps	
3 Internal finishes	3.1 Wall finishes incl. internal partitioning	
	3.2 Floor finishes	
	3.3 Ceiling finishes	
4 Fittings, furnishings and equipment	4.1 Building-related*	
	4.2 Non building-related**	
5 Services/MEP	5.1 Building-related* – HVAC incl. sanitary	
	5.2 Building-related* – lighting	
	5.3 Building-related* – lifts and escalators	
	5.4 Building-related* – safety, security and communication installations	
	5.5 Non building-related**	
6 Facade	6.1 External walls/opaque cladding	
	6.2 Curtain walling, windows and external doors	
7 External works	7.1 Roads, paths & pavings/hard landscaping	
	7.2 Soft landscaping	
	7.3 Fencing, railings and walls	
	7.4 External fixtures	
	7.5 External services incl. drainage	

*   Building-integrated technical systems and furniture, fittings and fixtures fixed to the building
**   Domestic, commercial and industrial appliances, e.g entertainment and office electronics, cooking appliances and loose furniture, fittings and fixtures. These items must not be included in the totals of the carbon calculations but only be stated separately in case non-building related items are part of the cost plan/BoQ

Table 6.01: Building components.
Source: SCP (Athina Papakosta)

Quantities measurement

Material quantities should be as per the project cost plan/bill of quantities, BIM model or as estimated from drawings. These should be in accordance with the RICS property measurement standards (2015) and the BCIS elemental standard form of cost analysis.[12]

Units of measurement to be reported

The unit for reporting the global warming potential/whole life carbon should be $kgCO_2e$ or suitable multiples thereof, eg tCO_2e. The carbon results should also be normalised in line with the project type, ie $kgCO_2e/m^2$ GIA for most building categories, $kgCO_2e/m3$ of internal building volume for storage and industrial units, etc.

Embodied carbon data sources

BS EN 15978 mandates that, 'Environmental information for the product stage is defined in the product EPD (EN 15804). If EPD unavailable, cradle-to-gate figures to be used calculated according to EN 15804.' There are several reliable data sources that are acceptable, such as Ecoinvent v3 onwards[13] and GaBi vXIV onwards.[14] These will help produce an 'embodied carbon factor' to be used for each material or component. As far as carbon conversion factors for fuel, refrigerants and water are concerned, the coefficients as issued by the government (BEIS) should be used.[15]

Table 6.01 represents the context for any assessment. The following sections address the modules/life stages as determined within BS EN 15978.

Modules A1-A3: product stage

The product stage carbon of the different elements should be calculated by assigning the respective suitable embodied carbon factors derived from the acceptable data sources identified in the table. **The calculation is: $kgCO_2e$ [A1-A3] = material quantity x material embodied carbon factor.**

Module A4: transport emissions (factory gate to site)

This is a question of identifying the transport types and the associated attributable emissions for delivery to site. These should be updated at the 'as built' stage to paint a more accurate picture, and therefore the contractor should be logging vehicle movements. **The calculation is: $kgCO_2e$ [A4] = material/system mass x transport distance x carbon conversion factor for fuel use.**

Module A5: construction/installation emissions

The carbon emissions from all onsite activities and plant accommodation should be covered. The average figure for construction site emissions of $1400kgCO_2e/£100k$ of project value, as provided by the relevant BRE SMARTWaste tool KPI (2015),[16] is suggested as a default for the 'as designed' stage. Appropriate allowances for site waste should be made. The site waste rates for different materials should be determined based on the standard wastage rates provided by the WRAP Net Waste tool at the 'as designed' stage.[17] At the 'as built' stage, both rates should be replaced with specific evidence-based site monitoring data provided by the contractor.

Module B: use stage

This stage should capture the carbon emissions associated with any building-related activities over the entire life cycle of the project, from practical completion to demolition. The intention is to measure and highlight to the design team the carbon impacts of design stage decisions post practical completion. Taking future uncertainty into account, sensible scenarios should be developed for the maintenance, repair, replacement, refurbishment and operation of the building. A life cycle analysis (LCA) is therefore an essential requirement.

Module B1: use stage emissions

This covers the release of GHGs from products and materials (eg refrigerants, paints, carpets) during the normal operation of the building. This type of data can be difficult to acquire, but can be accessed from product manufacturers, Health Performance Declaration certificates, EPDs or DEFRA.[18]

Module B2: maintenance emissions

The carbon emissions of all maintenance activities, including cleaning, should be taken into account. This includes impacts from associated energy and water use. Data for this can be sourced from facilities management/maintenance strategy reports, facade access and maintenance strategy, life cycle cost reports, O&M manuals and professional guidance, eg CIBSE Guide M.[19]

Modules B3-B4: repair and replacement emissions

This stage involves any emissions arising from the repair and replacement of relevant building components in line with sensible repair and replacement scenarios based on lifespan and further data from facilities management/maintenance strategy reports, facade access and maintenance strategy, life cycle cost reports, O&M manuals and professional guidance. The replacement emissions should capture all emissions associated with the supply of new products [A1-A5]. It should be noted that, for the purposes of consistency, it is assumed that repair, replacement and refurbishment use like-for-like replacements. An allowance should be made for future UK grid decarbonisation. While this is speculative, it does reflect a degree of future transition to a less carbon-intensive energy supply. See National Grid's Future Energy Scenarios.[20]

Module B5: refurbishment emissions

BS EN 15978 specifies that, 'Scenarios for refurbishment of the building, building elements and/or technical equipment shall be developed where details of planned refurbishment are known to the assessor. If no requirements for refurbishment are stated in the client's brief, the scenarios for refurbishment shall be typical for the type of building being assessed. The scenario for refurbishment shall describe all activities with environmental impacts and aspects arising from the refurbishment process.' The detailed life cycle analysis should assist with determining the likely refurbishment scenarios.

Module B6: operational energy use

All operational emissions from building-related systems should be included. This covers regulated energy consumption as per Part L (including heating, cooling, ventilation, domestic hot water, lighting and auxiliary systems) as projected throughout the life cycle of the project (excluding maintenance, repair, replacement and refurbishment). It should also include building integrated systems such as lift machinery, security systems, etc. All energy generating units such as solar thermal panels, wind turbines, gas boilers, Combined heat and power (CHP) and heat pumps should be included within the calculation. Data for this section is usually provided by the MEP consultants. Regulated energy use (as per Part L) is usually reported separately from unregulated energy use. It should be noted that the design stage modelled figures can vary from the actual 'in use' figures – hence the performance gap.

Module B7: operational water use

All carbon emissions relating to operational water consumption, both supply and waste, throughout the building's life cycle should be included. At the 'as designed' stage of the WLC assessment, estimates for water consumption should be based on the values provided in table 22 of the BSRIA's 'Rules of Thumb: Guidelines for the building services' (5th edition) for the respective building type.[21] These should be replaced with more accurate figures at the 'as built' stage.

Module C: end of life

The aim of this module is to get the design team to consider the selected materials and methods of construction from the perspective of their disposal or potential for reuse. With resource depletion and the circular economy coming to the fore, we need to understand the extent to which the carbon emissions of this stage can be mitigated by design stage considerations. Projecting into the future is difficult but, for consistency, the basic assumption is that processes will have the same carbon cost as they do today.

Module C1: deconstruction

This module includes all emissions associated with dismantling the building at the end of its life. A practical approach is to consider the overall construction emissions (A5) and treat the deconstruction as a percentage of this figure: a reasonable assumption could be 50%.

Module C2: transport

This refers to transport emissions arising from removing rubble from the building site and taking it to the disposal site. The guidance here is to research disposal sites nearest to the site and average the distance of the closest two. Then, as with A4, **$kgCO_2e$ [C2] = material/system mass × transport distance × carbon conversion factor for fuel use.**

Module C3: waste processing

Module C3 is directly linked to module D, and represents the carbon emissions costs of preparing materials for repurposing (reuse or recycling). C3 represents the carbon cost to bring the materials to the 'out-of-waste' state, whereas D represents the benefit. For example, removing mortar from a brick would be covered under C3 while the benefit of the brick reuse would be shown under D.

Module C4: disposal

This includes any emissions arising from landfilling or incinerating building components.

Module D: reuse, recovery, recycling stage

This module is described in BS EN 15978 as, 'Supplementary information beyond the building life cycle'. However, as noted above, with these issues coming to the fore through circular economic considerations, module D will be increasingly important in WLC assessments. Whereas modules A, B and C represent carbon costs over the life cycle of a building, module D represents future opportunities or benefits. If a material or system has the capacity for beneficial reuse, then this carbon credit can be captured within module D. The difficulty is that delivery is impossible to verify in advance. Nevertheless, designers need to be incentivised to deliver buildings that have a low carbon potential future when dismantled. This benefit, or offset, should be reported separately, as indicated by BS EN 15978. If a product such as brick is only capable of reuse as hardcore, then it can only be valued as such.

Compatibility with BREEAM

BREEAM 2014[22] includes 'introductory' elements (Mat 01 Life cycle impacts; Mat 04 Insulation; Mat 05 Durability and resilience; Ene 01 Reduction of energy use and carbon emissions; Wst 01 Construction waste management; Wst 02 Recycled aggregates) that are relevant to the whole life approach as per BS EN 15978. It is anticipated that the next iteration of BREEAM (2018) will cover embodied and whole life carbon reporting more thoroughly (see Introduction).

Life cycle analysis (LCA)

A life cycle analysis examines, at the design stage, a building's anticipated fabric and energy performance over its projected lifespan.

A detailed description of LCA can be found in:

- ISO 14040:2006 – LCA Principles and Framework
- ISO 14044:2006 – LCA Requirements and Guidelines

For the built environment an LCA can, as per the above ISOs, be summarised as a systematic set of procedures for compiling and examining the inputs and outputs of materials and energy, and the associated environmental impacts directly attributable to the functioning of a building throughout its life cycle.

For building designers this means developing, over all RIBA stages, an understanding of the impacts of their design decisions over the expected life of a building. The objectives are to optimise the efficient use of resources and minimise the environmental impacts of the building both during construction and throughout its life.

LCA is fundamental to a whole life carbon assessment. Understanding what happens to a building after practical completion is essential to designing low embodied carbon buildings. Design, as previously noted, should account for this from the outset. As a rough guide for large commercial buildings, the embodied carbon emissions over a 60-year period can be similar to those for constructing the building. The following LCAs illustrate key points.

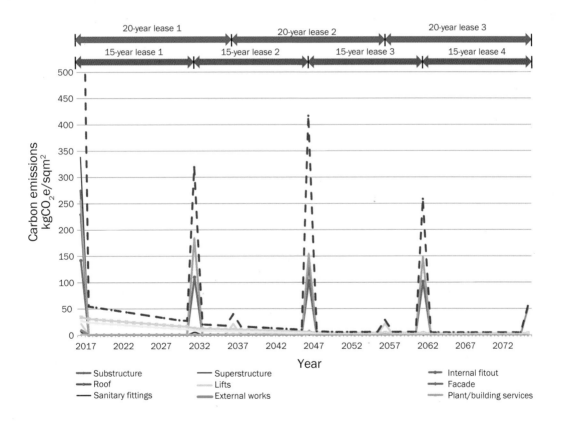

Figure 6.02: Carbon LCA of an office building showing replacement cycles aligned to 15-year lease cycles.

Figure 6.02 represents a planned LCA for an office building, showing when replacements are expected in line with a 15-year lease cycle (see case study 13 for a more realistic owner-occupier LCA). The horizontal axis is the passage of time; the vertical axis is the annual carbon cost for each of the categories shown. Along the top of the graph are the lease cycle options: 15 or 20 years.

This particular analysis has shown key replacements occurring consistent with a 15-year lease cycle. Life is seldom this tidy; however, what this shows is that the cladding, for example, is expected to be replaced at either 30 or 45 years. Double-glazed units tend to last around 35-40 years, which means that the best moment to replace the cladding from a carbon efficiency point of view would be between two lease events. More realistically, it will either be replaced earlier or possibly later than necessary. Both replacement options would be inefficient in material terms: the first because the cladding is being disposed of before the end of its useful life; the second because the system will start to fail past its expected life, meaning additional operational and maintenance carbon and financial costs. This graph also shows a neat correlation in the replacement of major items such as cladding, central plant roofs, etc. This will almost certainly prove to be optimistic.

An example of where LCAs could have helped understand future impacts is with many recent public buildings. These are often designed using office-type cladding systems, which have relatively short lifespans (40-50 years), and will result in high costs to the local authority when they need replacing. A proper initial LCA, projected over 60-100 years (a not unreasonable period for a public theatre or town hall) would ensure designers think long-term about the economic and social consequences of their choices. (See Chapter 2 on low carbon design choices and the Library of Birmingham.)

The next two graphs show the 15-year interior fitout life cycles of two different types of organisation, both within very large buildings. The first is an international bank; the second is a large technology company. Both LCAs are designed to inform interior fitout choices so as to minimise carbon emissions and optimise efficiency while responding to different corporate cultures. The LCAs start similarly but evolve very differently: the requirement for the bank is to minimise disruption, whereas constant change and reinvention is fundamental to the technology company's culture.

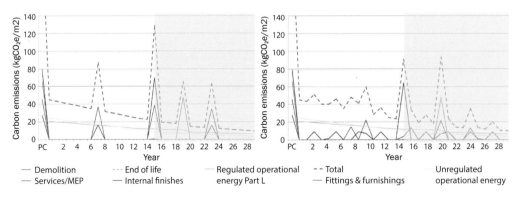

Figure 6.03: 15-year life cycle – interior fitout of an international bank v a large internet company.

What this shows is that there is no one answer to a low carbon requirement and, importantly, what needs to happen after practical completion. The occupiers' culture should inform the choices made at design stage.

Carbon and financial performance analysis

The carbon cost of component and system choices should be an important determining factor when designing a building. Most building owners, however, make decisions primarily based on financial cost. At SCP, we use two similar (but not to be confused) methods of assessing carbon cost v financial performance: MAC curves and carbon cost analysis.

MAC curves

Marginal abatement cost curves are otherwise known as MAC curves, or MACC. SCP uses these to compare the annualised relative operational carbon performance against the relative financial performance of disparate elements, such as double glazing, draught strips and mechanical controls. Such direct performance comparisons enable us to achieve the optimum operational/ financial combination.

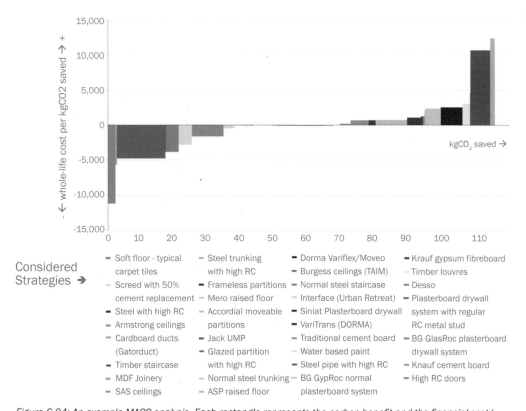

Considered Strategies →

- Soft floor - typical carpet tiles
- Screed with 50% cement replacement
- Steel with high RC
- Armstrong ceilings
- Cardboard ducts (Gatorduct)
- Timber staircase
- MDF Joinery
- SAS ceilings

- Steel trunking with high RC
- Frameless partitions
- Mero raised floor
- Accordial moveable partitions
- Jack UMP
- Glazed partition with high RC
- Normal steel trunking
- ASP raised floor

- Dorma Variflex/Moveo
- Burgess ceilings (TAIM)
- Normal steel staircase
- Interface (Urban Retreat)
- Siniat Plasterboard drywall
- VariTrans (DORMA)
- Traditional cement board
- Water based paint
- Steel pipe with high RC
- BG GypRoc normal plasterboard system

- Krauf gypsum fibreboard
- Timber louvres
- Desso
- Plasterboard drywall system with regular RC metal stud
- BG GlasRoc plasterboard drywall system
- Knauf cement board
- High RC doors

Figure 6.04: An example MACC analysis. Each rectangle represents the carbon benefit and the financial cost/ benefit of different elements of construction that affect environmental performance.

MAC curves are a visual method of ranking carbon reduction elements based on the amount of CO_2 they save against their cost per tonne of CO_2 saved. All those items that impact on environmental performance are shown so that they can be individually and collectively evaluated. The marginal abatement cost is plotted on the y-axis and the elements are ranked against this metric from lowest to highest. The width of the column is equal to the amount of carbon saved by the project, and the area of each column equal to the cost or benefit to the project. Items that are below the line are cost-efficient; items above the line are not.

Carbon cost analysis

SCP has developed a slightly different whole life carbon/cost (CC) tool. A CC analysis enables us to make comparisons between different design options on both financial and carbon cost terms over time. It takes into consideration both the initial construction carbon and financial costs of an element as well as the life cycle impacts of using it within the building fabric. For elements of construction such as cladding or fancoil units, the operational performance can be included. For these and similar examples, the comparison is between a combined embodied/operational carbon performance and a combined financial performance over the anticipated lifespan. Initial selections can then be made from a holistic, ie whole life, perspective on both financial and carbon terms.

This is obviously the most resource-efficient way to assess the design, assembly, use, and disposal of components. However, the costs of creating a building and the costs of its subsequent use are almost always seen as entirely separate. This may be understandable for developers, but it doesn't make sense for organisations that have a direct interest in the overall lifetime efficiency of a building (eg universities, airports, public buildings, etc). Yet such organisations still work to the 'lowest cost at practical completion' model, whatever the long-term implications, and the incentive for project managers is to deliver for lowest initial cost. Overall lifetime resource efficiency and a more circular approach will not be possible until there is a significant change in incentives and therefore culture.

Figure 6.05 is a simple CC analysis showing a comparison between five partition systems against an assumed baseline of plasterboard and metal stud. The analysis compares the supply and assembly of each system, and its use over a 15-year period. Plasterboard and stud is the zero point on both x and y axes. The horizontal dimension of each rectangle represents the carbon variation against the baseline, ie plasterboard and stud; the vertical dimension represents the financial cost or benefit. Both CO_2 and financial costs are assessed over this 15-year period, allowing for deterioration and a degree of replacement.

Carbon/cost analysis

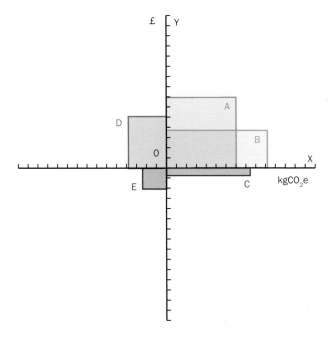

Figure 6.05: Carbon/cost analysis. This compares the carbon and cost performance of design options against a baseline. In this case various partition systems against plasterboard and stud.

- Items A and B show positive carbon and financial performance, with B better in carbon terms and A better financially. Both are a clear improvement on plasterboard and stud.
- Item C is a good carbon performer, but is just below the line financially. This may be worth a second look if the supplier can be persuaded to enhance the financial performance through cheaper units and/or through greater durability. Improved durability will reduce the repair/replacement occurrences and will therefore likely improve both carbon and cost performance.
- Item D is the second cheapest overall, but is the worst carbon performer.
- Item E is poor all around.

Conclusions

Using LCAs, MACC and CC analyses gives building designers a more sophisticated understanding of how their buildings will perform over their lifetime in terms of all CO_2e impacts. It is possible to compare not only between options but also between variants within an option, thus getting both a CO_2e and a financial understanding of the impacts of recycled content, procurement distances, relative durability, ease of demountability and different end of life scenarios.

Experience shows that LCAs, MACC and CC analyses go a long way to 'selling' environmentally-led design over and above the usual feel-good factors. Certainly, project managers and finance directors better understand low carbon thinking and the circular economy when provided with the hard data derived from these analyses.

CASE STUDY 13:

Life cycle analysis (LCA)

BY SIMON STURGIS

An LCA is a vital tool for whole life carbon management of a building over its anticipated life. Using an LCA informs design decisions made at the outset, and should be a basic tool for any design team. An LCA may also work in parallel with life cycle costing (LCC), which looks at the future cash flow of operating the building post completion.

This simple, user-friendly example LCA looks at the relative impacts of different parts of a building over 100 years. The building in question is an 80,000m² office scheme for an owner-occupier. The first LCA (shown in figure 6.06) is based on information from the design team at RIBA stage 3. The red diamonds show anticipated replacement cycles of the main components. This indicates a pretty chaotic future for the owner-occupier: after about 20 years, major work to the building is potentially required in a random sequence, meaning significant and uncoordinated replacement events. This is inefficient in both carbon and financial terms. Ideally these events would be grouped to allow for simultaneous replacements of major systems (lifts, plant/services, cladding), thereby minimising disruption.

The design team can use this information to develop a more carefully planned and less wasteful future life for the building. Through material and system specification choices, it is possible to adjust the timing of these events to produce a more synchronised future life cycle. By adopting circular economy thinking, it is also possible to plan for reuse and repurposing of elements that need replacing.

The dilemma for clients is that the aim should be for overall lifetime carbon and financial optimisation rather than focusing only on practical completion; however, we are all judged on the cost of a building on completion, even if it is not the cheapest lifetime solution.

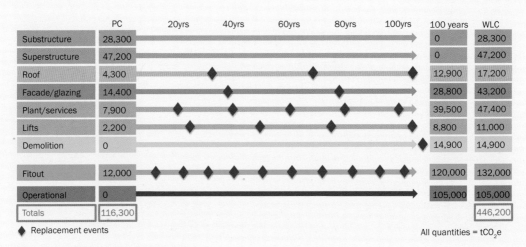

	PC	20yrs	40yrs	60yrs	80yrs	100yrs	100 years	WLC
Substructure	28,300						0	28,300
Superstructure	47,200						0	47,200
Roof	4,300						12,900	17,200
Facade/glazing	14,400						28,800	43,200
Plant/services	7,900						39,500	47,400
Lifts	2,200						8,800	11,000
Demolition	0						14,900	14,900
Fitout	12,000						120,000	132,000
Operational	0						105,000	105,000
Totals	116,300							446,200

♦ Replacement events

All quantities = tCO$_2$e

Figure 6.06: RIBA Stage 3: Whole life tCO$_2$e.

In the diagram above, the carbon cost of each item at practical completion (PC) is shown on the left. The largest item by far is the superstructure, at 47,200tCO$_2$e. The fitout is relatively minor, at 12,000tCO$_2$e. However, the WLC (whole life carbon) column shows that over 100 years the fitout has increased to 132,000tCO$_2$e (not including grid decarbonisation) due to regular retrofits, specified as occurring every ten years. The superstructure remains at 47,200tCO$_2$e as no work to it has been assumed. Therefore, fitout-related decisions made at design stage will have a far greater lifetime impact than the structure.

It is also worth noting the anticipated 105,000tCO$_2$e operational carbon emissions (regulated and unregulated). Over 100 years these represent only 29% of the total carbon emissions. For this building, the regulated emissions as per Part L are about half of the total operational emissions. This means that current legislation is only covering about 15% of this building's total carbon emissions. Also worth noting is that the initial construction carbon cost is approximately a quarter of the overall 100 years' carbon cost.

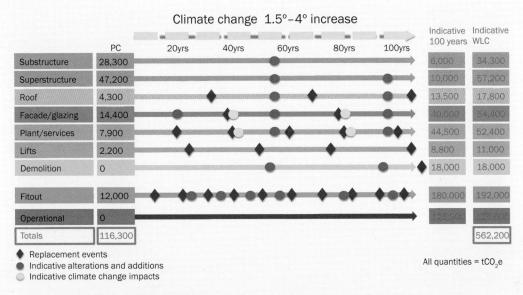

Figure 6.07: RIBA Stage 3: Whole life tCO$_2$e including future change scenario, and predicted climate change.

This next version of the diagram shows the predicted replacement cycles due to wear and tear as before, but includes two additional sets of carbon activities. The blue ovals illustrate changes due to imagined occupier requirements over 100 years, such as extensions, additions and alterations. The yellow ovals show possible impacts of climate change and consequent adaptations to plant/services and cladding. This shows a combination of planned and unplanned scenarios, with indicative figures for this on the right.

This more random mix is exactly what usually happens in the real world. Mapping out speculative future changes to the building helps us to understand the sort of pressures a building will come under in the future and enables a more flexible and responsive approach to the initial design. We may not wish to pay for future climate change today, and of course we don't know what future technology will be capable of, or what the occupiers will do, but we can at least ensure that these issues are given proper consideration now. We can also ensure that the building does not make future change difficult. This is not a new idea. The Empire State Building (completed in 1931) included in its brief the requirement to enable change by future generations. In 2010 it was refurbished and achieved LEED Gold Standard, something that couldn't have been predicted in 1931.

Conclusions

LCAs are an invaluable tool to ensure that we design for current and future resource optimisation. It is essential that design teams think proactively about post-practical completion. Key issues are maintenance, future replacement cycles and the impacts of climate change. In a sense, architects and engineers should think of themselves as designing a process rather than a finished building. When it comes to the future, one thing we can be sure of is that pressure on resources will increase; we need to think about this from the outset.

7

Conclusions – what's next?

The following are some concluding thoughts and predictions about embodied and whole life carbon (WLC) for the near future.

WLC assessment

Carbon emissions assessment, standards and ultimately legislation will evolve from considering solely operational emissions to whole life emissions. This will start with the launch of the InnovateUK project document, 'Whole Life Carbon Measurement: Implementation in the built environment', available through the UKGBC website. This will then evolve into the RICS Professional Statement in late 2017, followed quickly by BREEAM 2018, and will lead directly to planning authorities taking up WLC. Ultimately the Building Regulations will also have to take on board WLC, possibly through Allowable Solutions.

Life cycle analysis

LCA will become a vital part of good building design practice. It will enable designers to look past practical completion to the overall performance of the building over its intended life, and as such will be an essential design tool. Building purchasers will also require an LCA as part of the sales information to fully understand what they are taking on from the perspective of quality and the likely impacts of future climate change.

Carbon and money

Carbon cost analysis and marginal abatement cost curve analysis will become standard practice at design stage to ensure full cost/benefit analyses of the designers' carbon, cost and life cycle options are undertaken. This will provide economic understanding and authority to choices made.

Climate change

The impacts of future climate change will need to be understood and factored into design thinking and life cycle analysis as a matter of course. Buildings that are not immediately capable of managing the consequences of predicted temperature increases will at least need to be capable of economical future adaptation.

Circular economy

Circular economic thinking and optimising resource efficiency will become a key part of WLC-based design. Designing with recycled content will increase and designers will design for easy disassembly and reuse as standard.

Existing buildings

WLC analysis demonstrates the value of retaining and retrofitting existing structures and fabric. It also shows the value of building durable buildings. Georgian and Victorian housing units have proved a very good carbon investment given their long life. Will today's housing prove as resilient for the future? In many cases, the answer is probably not. In the context of climate change and diminishing resources, this is short-term thinking. Especially given our growing population, we need buildings to do their job for at least a century.

Health and wellbeing

Low carbon design must include the use of healthy materials, a healthy environment, and the wellbeing of the occupants. These principles work together and, in a sense, amplify each other to produce better buildings.

Improving WLC

There is still a lot to do to ensure a rigorous approach to WLC is in place. The RICS Professional Statement and BREEAM 2018 will be a start, but these will need to evolve. After all, operational assessment tools such as SAP, SBEM, EPCs and Part L calculations for planning are all notoriously inaccurate, despite many years of experience.

Industry's role

Industry will continue to lead in the evolution of WLC, the use of LCAs and engagement with circular economic principles. Standards and regulation will need to follow to maintain the pressure.

Data

Accessing reliable data will still be problematic. The likely solution will be to focus on a single database (BS EN 15804- and EPD-compliant) that is continually updated. This role was previously held by the Bath ICE database by Dr Craig Jones;[1] however, this has not been updated for many years and was not compatible with BS EN 15804 or current EPDs.

The role of architects

If they engage with WLC, architects will move to the centre of issues such as resource efficiency, LCA, low carbon buildings and the circular economy. All these issues come down to a better choice of materials, and better buildings. This, ultimately, is what architects are about.

Acknowledgements

[i] The ideas and work that are the substance of this book are the product of the group of people at Sturgis Carbon Profiling LLP, referred to within the text as 'SCP'.

Introduction

[1] Sturgis, S. and Roberts, G. (2010). Redefining Zero: Carbon profiling as a solution to whole life emission measurement in buildings. Sturgis Carbon Profiling. [online] Available at: http://sturgiscarbonprofiling.com/wp-content/uploads/2010/05/RICS.RedefiningZero.pdf [Accessed 16 Nov 2016]

[2] Macalister, T. (2011). Background: What caused the 1970s oil price shock? The Guardian. [online] Available at: https://www.theguardian.com/environment/2011/mar/03/1970s-oil-price-shock [Accessed 16 Nov 2016]

[3] The GreenAge (2015). How Building Regulations have tightened up over the last 50 years. [online] Available at: http://www.thegreenage.co.uk/building-regulations-changed-time/ [Accessed 16 Nov 2016]

[4] UK Ministry of Defence (2010). Global Strategic Trends Out to 2040. [online] Available at: https://www.gov.uk/government/uploads/system/uploads/attachment_data/file/33717/GST4_v9_Feb10.pdf [Accessed 16 Nov 2016]

[5] HM Government (2009). The UK Low Carbon Transition Plan: National strategy for climate and energy. [online] Available at: https://www.gov.uk/government/uploads/system/uploads/attachment_data/file/228752/9780108508394.pdf [Accessed 18 Nov 2016]

[6] Helm, D. (2013). The Carbon Crunch: How We're Getting Climate Change Wrong – and How to Fix it. Yale University Press.

[7] ISO: International Organization for Standardization (2016). ISO 14000 – Environmental management. [online] Available at: http://www.iso.org/iso/iso14000 [Accessed 18 Nov 2016]

[8] CEN: European Committee for Standardization (2014). CEN/TC 350 – Sustainability of construction works. [online] Available at: https://standards.cen.eu/dyn/www/f?p=204:7:0::::FSP_ORG_ID:481830&cs=181BD0E0E925FA84EC4B8BCCC284577F8 [Accessed 18 Nov 2016]

[9] BSI: British Standards Institution (2011). BS EN 15978:2011 – Sustainability of construction works; Assessment of environmental performance of buildings: Calculation method. [online] Available at: http://shop.bsigroup.com/ProductDetail/?pid=000000000030256638 [Accessed 18 Nov 2016]

[10] BSI: British Standards Institution (2013). BS EN 15804:2012+A1:2013 – Sustainability of construction works; Environmental product declarations: Core rules for the product category of construction products. [online] Available at: http://shop.bsigroup.com/ProductDetail/?pid=000000000030279721 [Accessed 18 Nov 2016]

[11] This team was led by the author, and included Sturgis Carbon Profiling, Arup, Atkins, Sustainable Business Partnership, Land Securities, Laing O'Rourke, Cambridge University, and the Royal Institute of Chartered Surveyors (RICS). It was supported by the UKGBC, Argent, Grosvenor, Legal & General, M&S, Derwent London, HS2, and Higgins.

[12] International Living Future Institute (2017). Living Building Challenge. [online] Available at: https://living-future.org/lbc/ [Accessed 23 Jan 2017]

Chapter 1

[1] HM Government (2008). Climate Change Act 2008. [online] Available at: http://www.legislation.gov.uk/ukpga/2008/27/pdfs/ukpga_20080027_en.pdf [Accessed 5 Dec 2016]

[2] HM Government (2009). The UK Low Carbon Transition Plan: National strategy for climate and energy. [online] Available at: https://www.gov.uk/government/uploads/system/uploads/attachment_data/file/228752/9780108508394.pdf [Accessed 18 Nov 2016]

[3] HM Government (2010). Low Carbon Construction – Innovation & Growth Team: Final report. [online] Available at: https://www.gov.uk/government/uploads/system/uploads/attachment_data/file/31773/10-1266-low-carbon-construction-IGT-final-report.pdf [Accessed 18 Nov 2016]

[4] Carrington, D. (2012). George Osborne's attacks on the environment are costing UK billions. The Guardian. [online] Available at: https://www.theguardian.com/environment/damian-carrington-blog/2012/mar/15/george-osborne-budget-bill-uk [Accessed 16 Nov 2016]

[5] Lockie, S., Berebecki, P. and Faithful+Gould (2014). RICS Professional Guidance, Global: Methodology to calculate embodied carbon. [online] 1st edition, fig 4. Available at: http://www.rics.org/Global/Methodology_to_calculate_embodied_carbon_1st_edition_PGguidance_2014.pdf [Accessed 16 Nov 2016]

[6] Clark, D. (2013). What Colour is Your Building? Measuring and Reducing the Energy and Carbon Footprint of Buildings. RIBA Publishing.

[7] RIBA and CIBSE (2016). Carbon Buzz. [online] Available at: http://www.carbonbuzz.org/ [Accessed 17 Nov 2016]

[8] EPA: US Environmental Protection Agency (2016). Future of Climate Change. [online] Available at: https://www.epa.gov/climate-change-science/future-climate-change [Accessed 17 Nov 2016]

Chapter 2

[1] RIBA (2013). RIBA Plan of Work 2013 – Stages. [online] Available at: https://www.architecture.com/files/ribaprofessionalservices/practice/ribaplanofwork2013template.pdf [Accessed 28 Nov 2016]

[2] Papakosta, A. (2016). Whole-life Carbon: Structural systems. Building. [online] Available at: http://www.building.co.uk/whole-life-carbon-structural-systems/5081262.article [Accessed 17 Nov 2016]

[3] Cheung, L. and Farnetani, M. (2015). Whole-life carbon: Facades. Building. [online] Available at: http://www.building.co.uk/whole-life-carbon-facades/5078620.article [Accessed 18 Nov 2016]

Chapter 3

[1] The Ellen MacArthur Foundation (2015). Circular Economy Overview. [online] Available at: https://www.ellenmacarthurfoundation.org/circular-economy/overview/concept [Accessed 17 Nov 2016]

[2] Gordon, A. (1972). Designing for Survival: The President introduces his long life/loose fit/low energy study. RIBA Journal.

[3] Stuart, C. (2013). Whole-life Carbon: Domestic. Building. [online] Available at: http://www.building.co.uk/whole-life-carbon-domestic/5056579.article [Accessed 18 Nov 2016]

[4] National Grid – Future Energy Scenarios. July 2015

[5] Roberts, G., Dwyer, P. and Taylor, J. (2011). Non-domestic Real Estate Climate Change Model. RICS. [online] Available at: http://sturgiscarbonprofiling.com/wp-content/uploads/2011/07/RICS.Climate-Risk-Model.pdf [Accessed 17 Nov 2016]

[6] Lafuente, J., Darviris, T. and Roberts, G. (2015). European Climatic Risk Toolkit. RICS. [online] Available at: http://www.rics.org/uk/knowledge/research/research-reports/climatic-risk-toolkit/ [Accessed 18 Nov 2016]

[7] Guermanova, M. and Arora, P. (2015). Whole-life Carbon: Retrofit vs EnerPHit. Building. [online] Available at: http://www.building.co.uk/whole-life-carbon-retrofit-vs-enerphit/5076176.article [Accessed 17 Nov 2016]

[8] UK Department of Energy & Climate Change (2016). Annual domestic energy bills. [online] Available at: https://www.gov.uk/government/statistical-data-sets/annual-domestic-energy-price-statistics [Accessed 17 Nov 2016]

[9] Johnston, D., Farmer, D., Brooke-Peat, M. and Miles-Shenton, D. (2014). Bridging the Domestic Building Fabric Performance Gap. Building Research & Information, [online] Volume 44(2). Available at: http://www.tandfonline.com/doi/abs/10.1080/09613218.2014.979093?journalCode=rbri20 [Accessed 17 Nov 2016]

Chapter 4

[1] Lafuente, J., Darviris, T. and Roberts, G. (2015). European Climatic Risk Toolkit. RICS. [online] Available at: http://www.rics.org/uk/knowledge/research/research-reports/climatic-risk-toolkit/ [Accessed 18 Nov 2016]

[2] Grosvenor (2016). Living Cities: Our approach in practice. [online] Available at: http://www.grosvenor.com/downloads/living-cities-our-approach-in-practice.pdf [Accessed 18 Nov 2016]

[3] Salvo (2016). Salvo Web: Gateway to the world of architectural salvage. [online] Available at: http://www.salvo.co.uk/ [Accessed 18 Nov 2016]

[4] Recipro UK Ltd (2016). Recipro. [online] Available at: http://www.recipro-uk.com/ [Accessed 17 Nov 2016]

[5] Lafuente, J., Darviris, T. and Roberts, G. (2015). European Climatic Risk Toolkit. RICS. [online] Available at: http://www.rics.org/uk/knowledge/research/research-reports/climatic-risk-toolkit/ [Accessed 18 Nov 2016]

[6] Roberts, G. and Lafuente, J. (2013). Whole-life Carbon: Airports. Building. [online] Available at: http://www.building.co.uk/whole-life-carbon-airports/5063616.article [Accessed 18 Nov 2016]

[7] UK Department for Transport (2013). UK Aviation Forecasts. [online] Available at: https://www.gov.uk/government/uploads/system/uploads/attachment_data/file/223839/aviation-forecasts.pdf [Accessed 18 Nov 2016]

[8] CAA: Civil Aviation Authority (2014). CAA Passenger Survey Report 2014. [online] Available at: https://www.caa.co.uk/uploadedFiles/CAA/Content/Standard_Content/Data_and_analysis/Datasets/Passenger_survey/CAA%20Passenger%20Survey%20Report%202014.pdf [Accessed 18 Nov 2016]

Chapter 5

[1] Berners-Lee, M. (2010). How Bad are Bananas? The Carbon Footprint of Everything. London: Profile.

[2] Lafuente, J. and Darviris, T. (2014). Whole-life Carbon: Lifestyle. Building. [online] Available at: http://www.building.co.uk/whole-life-carbon-lifestyle/5072114.article [Accessed 18 Nov 2016]

[3] Berners-Lee, M. (2010). How Bad are Bananas? The Carbon Footprint of Everything. London: Profile.

Chapter 6

[1] BSI: British Standards Institution (2011). BS EN 15978:2011 – Sustainability of construction works; Assessment of environmental performance of buildings: Calculation method. [online] Available at: http://shop.bsigroup.com/ProductDetail/?pid=000000000030256638 [Accessed 18 Nov 2016]

[2] BSI: British Standards Institution (2013). BS EN 15804:2012+A1:2013 – Sustainability of construction works; Environmental product declarations: Core rules for the product category of construction products. [online] Available at: http://shop.bsigroup.com/ProductDetail/?pid=000000000030279721 [Accessed 18 Nov 2016]

[3] HM Government (2009). The UK Low Carbon Transition Plan: National strategy for climate and energy. [online] Available at: https://www.gov.uk/government/uploads/system/uploads/attachment_data/file/228752/9780108508394.pdf [Accessed 18 Nov 2016]

[4] HM Government (2009). Low Carbon Industrial Strategy: A vision. [online] Available at: https://www.gov.uk/government/uploads/system/uploads/attachment_data/file/243628/978777714698X.pdf [Accessed 18 Nov 2016]

[5] UK Department for Environment, Food & Rural Affairs (2009). Guidance on how to measure and report your greenhouse gas emissions. [online] Available at: https://www.gov.uk/government/publications/guidance-on-how-to-measure-and-report-your-greenhouse-gas-emissions [Accessed 18 Nov 2016]

[6] BSI: British Standards Institution (2011). BS EN 15978:2011 – Sustainability of construction works; Assessment of environmental performance of buildings: Calculation method. [online] Available at: http://shop.bsigroup.com/ProductDetail/?pid=000000000030256638 [Accessed 18 Nov 2016]

[7] CEN: European Committee for Standardization (2014). CEN/TC 350 – Sustainability of construction works. [online] Available at: https://standards.cen.eu/dyn/www/f?p=204:7:0::::FSP_ORG_ID:481830&cs=181BD0E0E925FA84EC4B8BCCC284577F8 [Accessed 18 Nov 2016]

[8] BSI: British Standards Institution (2011). PAS 2050:2011 – Specification for the assessment of the life cycle greenhouse gas emissions of goods and services. [online] Available at: http://shop.bsigroup.com/en/forms/PASs/PAS-2050/ [Accessed 18 Nov 2016]

[9] BSI: British Standards Institution (2016). PAS 2080:2016 – Carbon management in infrastructure. [online] Available at: http://shop.bsigroup.com/ProductDetail?pid=000000000030323493 [Accessed 18 Nov 2016]

[10] ISO: International Organization for Standardization (2016). ISO 14000 – Environmental management. [online] Available at: http://www.iso.org/iso/iso14000 [Accessed 18 Nov 2016]

[11] RICS: Royal Institution of Chartered Surveyors (2015). RICS Property Measurement. [online] Available at: http://www.rics.org/uk/knowledge/professional-guidance/professional-statements/rics-property-measurement-1st-edition/ [Accessed 24 Jan 2016]

[12] RICS: Royal Institution of Chartered Surveyors (2013). BCIS Elemental Standard Form of Cost Analysis. [online] Available at: https://www.rics.org/uk/knowledge/bcis/about-bcis/forms-and-documents/bcis-elemental-standard-form-of-cost-analysis/ [Accessed 24 Jan 2016]

[13] Ecoinvent (2013). The Ecoinvent database. [online] Available at: http://www.ecoinvent.org/[Accessed 24 Jan 2016]

[14] Thinkstep (2016). GaBi LCA Databases. [online] Available at: http://www.gabi-software.com/databases/gabi-databases/ [Accessed 24 Jan 2016]

[15] UK Department for Business, Energy & Industrial Strategy (2016). Greenhouse gas reporting – Conversion factors 2016. [online] Available at: https://www.gov.uk/government/publications/greenhouse-gas-reporting-conversion-factors-2016 [Accessed 24 Jan 2016]

[16] BRE: Building Research Establishment (2015). SMARTWaste. [online] Available at: www.smartwaste.co.uk [Accessed 24 Jan 2016]

[17] WRAP: Waste and Resources Action Programme (2017). Net Waste Tool. [online] Available at: http://nwtool.wrap.org.uk/ [Accessed 24 Jan 2016]

[18] UK Department for Environment, Food & Rural Affairs (2009). Guidance on how to measure and report your greenhouse gas emissions. [online] Available at: https://www.gov.uk/government/publications/guidance-on-how-to-measure-and-report-your-greenhouse-gas-emissions [Accessed 18 Nov 2016]

[19] CIBSE: Chartered Institution of Building Services Engineers (2014). GVM/14 CIBSE Guide M: Maintenance Engineering & Management. [online] Available at: http://www.cibse.org/Knowledge/knowledge-items/detail?id=a0q20000008I7oZAAS [Accessed 24 Jan 2016]

[20] National Grid plc (2016). Future Energy Scenarios. [online] Available at: http://fes.nationalgrid.com/fes-document/ [Accessed 5 Dec 2016]

[21] BSRIA: Building Services Research and Information Association (2011). Rules of Thumb – Guidelines for building services (BG 9/2011). [online] 5th edition. Available at: https://www.bsria.co.uk/information-membership/bookshop/publication/rules-of-thumb-guidelines-for-building-services-5th-edition/[Accessed 24 Jan 2016]

[22] BRE: Building Research Establishment (2017). BREEAM: Building Research Establishment Environmental Assessment Method. [online] Available at: http://www.breeam.com/ [Accessed 24 Jan 2016]

Chapter 7

[1] Jones, C. and Hammond, G. (2004). Inventory of Carbon and Energy (ICE). [online] Available at: http://www.environmenttools.co.uk/directory/tool/name/bath-university-inventory-of-carbon-and-energy-ice-dataset/id/780 [Accessed 18 Nov 2016]

* Figure 1.01: Carbon Brief (2015). Data Dashboard: Energy consumption by country in 2014 (all fuel sources). [online] Available at: https://www.carbonbrief.org/data-dashboard-energy [Accessed 16 Nov 2016]

** Table 1.01: IPCC: Intergovernmental panel on climate change (2007). Climate Change 2007 – Working Group I: The Physical Science Basis – 2.10.2 Direct Global Warming Potentials. [online] Available at: https://www.ipcc.ch/publications_and_data/ar4/wg1/en/ch2s2-10-2.html [Accessed 16 Nov 2016]

GLOSSARY

Allowable solutions
Allowable solutions are part of the government's strategy for the delivery of mainstream zero carbon new homes from 2016. Through the mechanism of Allowable Solutions, the carbon emissions which can not be cost-effectively offset on site after carbon compliance has been achieved, will be tackled through nearby or remote measures. (Adapted from Zero Carbon Hub website)

Anaerobic digestion
Natural process in which microorganisms break down organic matter, in the absence of oxygen, into biogas (a mixture of carbon dioxide (CO_2) and methane) and digestate (a nitrogen-rich fertiliser). The biogas can be used directly in engines for combined heat and power (CHP), burned to produce heat, or can be cleaned and used in the same way as natural gas or as a vehicle fuel. (Adapted from DECC and DEFRA Anaerobic Digestion Strategy and Action Plan)

Anthropogenic carbon emissions
Portion of carbon dioxide in the atmosphere that is produced directly by human activities, such as the burning of fossil fuels, rather than by such processes as respiration and decay. (Adapted from American Heritage Science Dictionary)

Big data
Data sets, typically consisting of billions or trillions of records, that are so vast and complex that they require new and powerful computational resources to process. (Based on Random House Dictionary)

BREEAM
Building Research Establishment's Environmental Assessment Method is a sustainability rating scheme for the built environment focused on sustainability in building design, construction and use. Its main aims include mitigating the life cycle impacts of buildings on the environment, enabling buildings to be recognised according to their environmental benefits, providing a credible, environmental label for buildings and to stimulating demand and creating value for sustainable buildings, building products and supply chains. (Adapted from BREEAM In-Use International Technical Manual)

Building emission rate
Building carbon emissions rate (BER) expressed as $kgCO_2/m^2$ per year. This refers to operational emissions only. (Adapted from UK Building Regulations – Part L2A)

Capital carbon emissions
See 'Embodied carbon'

Carbon
The terms 'carbon' or 'carbon emissions', as used in this book, are shorthand for 'carbon dioxide or equivalent greenhouse gas emissions', ie CO_2e. See 'Carbon dioxide equivalent'

Carbon budget
A 'carbon budget' is the assessment of the total whole life carbon emissions attributable to a project as assessed at the design stages. As with a financial budget, the carbon budget can be managed and adjusted over the course of a project.

Carbon dioxide
A colourless, odourless gas produced by burning carbon and organic compounds and by respiration. It is naturally present in air (about 0.03 per cent) and is absorbed by plants in photosynthesis. (Adapted from The Law Dictionary)

Carbon dioxide equivalent
Measure used to compare the emissions from various greenhouse gases based on their global warming potential. For example, the global warming potential for methane over 100 years is 21. This means that emissions of one metric tonnes of methane is equivalent to emissions of 21 metric tonnes of carbon dioxide. The unit of measurement is carbon dioxide equivalents (kg CO_2e). (Adapted from OECD). Its abbreviation in the text to 'carbon' is to aid readability.

Carbon emissions
See 'Carbon'

Carbon footprint
The amount of carbon dioxide released into the atmosphere as a result of the activities of a particular individual, organisation or community. (Oxford Dictionary) This can also apply to a building, a component or a system.

Circular economy
A circular economy is restorative and regenerative by design, and aims to keep products, components and materials at their highest utility and value at all times. The objective is to optimise reuse of materials, and minimise waste by maximising opportunities for reuse and recycling. (Adapted from the Ellen MacArthur Foundation)

Circularity
See 'Circular economy'

Climate change
A change in global or regional climate patterns, in particular a change apparent from the mid to late 20th century onwards and attributed largely to the increased levels of atmospheric carbon dioxide produced by the use of fossil fuels. (Oxford Dictionary)

Code for Sustainable Homes	The Code for Sustainable Homes (the Code) is an environmental assessment method for rating and certifying the performance of new homes. It is a national standard for use in the design and construction of new homes with a view to encouraging continuous improvement in sustainable home building. (Code for Sustainable Homes. Technical Guide)
Conservation area	Conservation areas are designated to safeguard areas of special architectural and historic interest, the character and appearance of which it is desirable to preserve or enhance. (City of London website)
Construction process (embodied carbon stages)	The construction process stage covers all processes that occur on site up to the practical completion of the construction work. This would be covered by Module A5 of BS EN 15978. (Adapted from BS EN 15978: 2011)
Cooling load	Amount of heat energy that would need to be removed from a space (cooling) to maintain the temperature within an acceptable range. (BASIX, Government of New South Wales)
Decarbonisation	Decarbonisation denotes the declining average carbon intensity of primary energy over time. (IPCC – Working Group III)
Design and build contract	Construction projects where the contractor carries out both the design and the construction work. (Adapted from JCT Contracts)
Dwelling emission rate	Dwelling carbon emissions rate expressed as $kgCO_2/m^2$ per year. (Adapted from UK Building Regulations – Part L1A)
Embedded carbon emissions	See 'Embodied carbon'
Embodied carbon	Carbon emissions that are the consequence of: the sourcing of raw material, transportation to a factory, fabrication into components and systems, delivery to site, and assembly into a finished building. Following completion, embodied emissions also refer to maintenance and replacement over an assumed building life expectancy and final disassembly and disposal.
End of life (embodied carbon stages)	The end-of-life stage of a building starts when the building is decommissioned and is not intended to have any further use. At this point, the building's demolition/deconstruction may be considered as a multi-output process that provides a source of materials, products and building elements that are to be discarded, recovered, recycled or reused. This would be covered by Modules C1 to C4 of BS EN 15978. (Adapted from BS EN 15978: 2011)
Energy Performance Certificate	Official document compulsory in the UK for any property being sold, rented or built. EPCs contains information about the property's energy use and typical energy costs and recommendations about how to reduce energy use and save money. An EPC gives a property an energy efficiency rating from A (most efficient) to G (least efficient) and is valid for 10 years. (Adapted from Gov.UK)
EnerPHit	Established standard for refurbishment of existing buildings using PassivHaus components. (Adapted from PassivHaus Institute)
Environmental product declaration	An EPD communicates verifiable, accurate, non-misleading environmental information for products and their applications, thereby supporting scientifically based, fair choices and stimulating the potential for market-driven continuous environmental improvement. The standardisation process has taken place in accordance with EN ISO 14025. (Adapted from BS EN 15804: 2012)
European Union Emissions Trading System	The EU Emissions Trading System (EU ETS) is a cornerstone of the EU's policy to combat climate change and its key tool for reducing greenhouse gas emissions cost-effectively. It is the world's first major carbon market and remains the biggest one. (Adapted from the European Commission website)
FSC certification	Certification scheme for forest owners and managers to demonstrate that they are managing their forests responsibly. (Adapted from FSC website)
Geographic information system	A geographic information system (GIS) is a computer system for capturing, storing, managing and displaying data related to any element on the Earth's surface like rivers or trees, but also buildings, properties, roads, brownfields, etc. GIS can show on one map many different kinds of data linked to each of these elements – expected value, carbon intensity, tenancy, sustainability accreditation, age, etc. This enables people to more easily see, analyse and understand patterns and relationships. (Adapted from National Geographic Society)
GHG scopes	Greenhouse gas emissions are categorised into three groups or 'scopes' by the most widely-used international accounting tool, the Greenhouse Gas (GHG) Protocol. While scope 1 (eg fuel used in company vehicles) and 2 cover direct emissions sources and purchased electricity, scope 3 emissions cover all indirect emissions due to the activities of an organisation. These include emissions from both suppliers and consumers. (Adapted from GHG Protocol)

Global warming potential	The global warming potential provides a common unit of measure that allows comparisons of the global warming impacts of different gases. Specifically, it is a measure of how much energy the emissions of 1 tonnes of a gas will absorb over a given period of time, relative to the emissions of 1 tonnes of carbon dioxide (CO_2). The larger the GWP, the more that a given gas warms the Earth compared to CO_2 over that time period. The time period usually used for GWPs is 100 years. CO_2, by definition, has a GWP of 1. (Adapted from the US Environmental Protection Agency)
Ground granulated blast-furnace slag	By-product of iron and steel-making obtained from a blast furnace in water or steam, used in concrete in combination with Portland cement as part of a blended cement. Ground granulated slag reacts with water to produce cementitious properties.
Healthy materials Red List	The Red List contains the worst-in-class materials prevalent in the building industry. The commonly used chemicals on the Red List are: Polluting the environment, Bio-accumulating up the food chain until they reach toxic concentrations, Harming construction and factory workers. (Adapted from Living Future) See 'Living Building Challenge'
Heating load	Amount of heat energy that would need to be added to a space to maintain the temperature within an acceptable range. (BASIX, Government of New South Wales)
Innovate UK	Innovate UK is the UK government's innovation agency, an executive non-departmental public body, sponsored by the Department for Business, Energy & Industrial Strategy. With a strong business focus, Innovate UK drives growth by working with companies to de-risk, enable and support innovation. (Adapted from Gov.UK)
In use (embodied carbon stages)	The in use stage covers the period from the practical completion of the construction work to the point of time when the building is deconstructed/demolished. This would be covered by Modules B1 to B5 of BS EN 15978. (Adapted from BS EN 15978: 2011)
Life cycle analysis	Compilation and evaluation of the inputs, outputs and the potential environmental impacts of a product system throughout its life cycle (Adapted from BS EN 15804: 2012)
Linear economy	'Take, make, dispose' economic model that relies on large quantities of cheap, easily accessible materials and energy. This is how most economies work, depending on constant supply of new material, and the consequent vast quantities of post-use waste. (Adapted from the Ellen MacArthur Foundation)
Listed buildings	In the UK, a 'listed building' is a building, object or structure that has been judged to be of national importance in terms of architectural or historic interest and included on a special register, called the List of Buildings of Special Architectural or Historic Interest. (Adapted from the Planning Portal)
Living Building Challenge	Accreditation scheme devised by the International Living Future Institute based in Seattle, aiming to create buildings that give more than they take and are: - Regenerative spaces that connect occupants to light, air, food, nature, and community. - Self-sufficient and remain within the resource limits of their site. Living Buildings produce more energy than they use and collect and treat all water on site. - Creating a positive impact on the human and natural systems that interact with them. - Places that last. Living Buildings need to be designed to operate for a hundred years' time. - Healthy and beautiful. (Adapted from Living Future website)
Operational carbon	This term relates to the carbon emissions that arise during the use (ie operation) of a building from the lighting, heating, ventilation, cooling and power used in day-to-day activities. This would be covered by Module B6 of BS EN 15978. (Adapted from BCO/SCP)
PassivHaus	Passivhaus is an advanced building standard whose target is a building with a high level of occupant comfort and very little energy use, achieved with highly efficient thermal performance, exceptional airtightness and mechanical ventilation.
Planning application	In the UK, a planning application is a formal request to a local authority for permission to build something new or to add something to an existing building. (Adapted from Collins Dictionary)
Post-occupancy evaluation	Post-occupancy evaluation (PoE) is the process of obtaining feedback on a building's performance in use, aiming to highlight any immediate teething problems that can be addressed and solved; identify any gaps in communication and understanding that impact on the building operation; provide lessons that can be used to improve design and procurement on future projects and act as a benchmarking aid to compare across projects and over time. It is the author's view that any PoE should also include a review of building fabric performance, for example the maintenance and replacement cycles in relation to those anticipated. (Adapted from BRE website)

Product (embodied carbon stages)	This covers the 'cradle to gate' processes for the materials and services used in the construction; the rules for determining their impacts and aspects are defined in EN 15804. The 'product' stage in BS EN 15978 is covered by modules A1 to A3. (Adapted from BS EN 15978: 2011)
Regulated operational energy/emissions	These are building-related carbon emissions that are controlled by various statutory requirements, such as building control through Part L of the Building Regulations. Regulated emissions arise predominantly from the heating, lighting and cooling of a building. (Adapted from BCO/SCP)
RIBA Plan of Work 2013	The RIBA Plan of Work 2013 organises the process of briefing, designing, constructing, maintaining, operating and using building projects into a number of key stages. It details the tasks and outputs required at each stage, which may vary or overlap to suit specific project requirements. (Adapted from RIBA Plan of Work 2013 – Overview)
RIBA stages	See 'RIBA Plan of Work 2013'
Section 106	Planning obligations focused on site-specific mitigation of the impact of development. S106 agreements are often referred to as 'developer contributions' along with highway contributions and the Community Infrastructure Levy. The common uses of planning obligations are to secure affordable housing, and to specify the type and timing of this housing; and to secure financial contributions to provide infrastructure or affordable housing. (Adapted from PAS)
Sequestration	A natural or artificial process by which carbon dioxide is removed from the atmosphere and held in solid or liquid form. (Oxford Dictionaries) This is frequently used in relation to the CO_2 'locked' within timber.
Simplified Building Energy Model (SBEM)	Software tool that provides an analysis of a building's energy consumption. SBEM is used for non-domestic buildings in support of the National Calculation Methodology (NCM), the Energy Performance of Buildings Directive (EPBD) and the Green Deal. (Adapted from BRE)
Standard Assessment Procedure (SAP)	The Standard Assessment Procedure (SAP) is the methodology used by the government to assess and compare the energy and environmental performance of dwellings. Its purpose is to provide accurate and reliable assessments of dwelling energy performances that are needed to underpin energy and environmental policy initiatives. (Adapted from Gov.UK)
Supply chain	Interconnected hierarchy of supply contracts necessary to procure a built asset. Managing the supply chain involves understanding the breakdown and traceability of products and services, organisations, logistics, people, activities, information and resources that transform raw materials into a finished product that is fit for its purpose. (Adapted from Designing Buildings website)
Tier 1 and Tier 2 subcontractors	Subcontractors work at a variety of levels. The primary, or general, contractor works directly with the customer. The primary contractor hires first-tier contractors to perform work on the customer's project. The second-tier contractor is hired by the first-tier contractor to perform specific tasks. (Adapted from Chron)
Unregulated operational energy/emissions	These are building-related carbon emissions that are not controlled by statutory requirements, such as the emissions arising from the use of small power, fridges, TV's, computers, kettles, sound systems, etc.
U-value	The U-value signifies the heat lost through a given thickness of a particular material.The best insulating materials have a U-value of close to zero – the lower the better. (Adapted from The Green Age)
Whole life carbon	A whole life carbon assessment takes account of all the carbon emissions associated with creating and using a building over its lifespan. This includes the carbon associated with the production of construction materials, their transport and assembly on site, the emissions associated with a building's activities in use, including maintenance and repair, and the building's eventual disassembly.
Zero carbon	As currently used in relation to the built environment, a 'zero carbon' building is one that is able to reduce operational carbon emissions to a minimum and offset the remaining emissions, thus equalling 'zero' emissions. The author believes that this term is incorrect and misleading, because when embodied carbon emissions are also considered there are very few buildings that can be said to make zero carbon impact on the environment.

ACRONYMS

ACA	Airport Carbon Accreditation	GIS	Geographic information system
ACI	Airports Council International	GLULAM	Glued laminated timber
AI	Artificial intelligence	GWP	Global warming potential
BEIS	Department for Business, Energy & Industrial Strategy	HM	Her/His Majesty's
BER	Building emission rate	HS2	High Speed Two Limited
BIM	Building information modelling	ICE	Inventory of Carbon and Energy
BIS	Department for Business Innovation and Skills	IGT	Innovation and Growth Team
BOS	Blast oxygen furnaces	ISO	International Organization for Standardization
BRE	Building Research Establishment	IWLCIB	Implementing whole life carbon in buildings
BREEAM	Building Research Establishment Environmental Assessment Method	KPI	Key Performance Indicator
BS	British Standards	LCA	Life cycle analysis
BS EN	British Standard European Norm	LLP	Limited liability partnership
BSI	British Standards Institution	LST	Liverpool Street Station
CAA	Civil Aviation Authority	M&S	Marks & Spencer
CC	Carbon cost	MAC	Marginal abatement cost
CCA	Carbon cost analysis	O&M	Operation and maintenance
CEN TC	European Committee for Standardization Technical Committee	OBE	Order of the British Empire
CFC	Chlorofluorocarbon	OC	Operational carbon
CIBSE	Chartered Institution of Building Services Engineers	PAD	Paddington Station
		PAX	Passengers
CLT	Cross-laminated timber	PFA	Pulverised fuel ash
CO_2	Carbon dioxide	PoE	Post-occupancy evaluation
CO_2e	Carbon dioxide equivalent	PPC	Polyester powder coated
CSR	Corporate social responsibility	PT RC	Post-tensioned and reinforced concrete
DECC	Department of Energy & Climate Change	PV	Photovoltaic
DEFRA	Department for Environment, Food & Rural Affairs	RC	Reinforced concrete
DER	Dwelling emission rate	RIBA	Royal Institute of British Architects
EAF	Electric arc furnaces	RICS	Royal Institute of Chartered Surveyors
EC	Embodied carbon	SAP	Standard Assessment Procedure
ECF	European Climate Foundation	SBEM	Simplified Building Energy Model
EoL	End of life	SCP	Sturgis Carbon Profiling
EPC	Energy Performance Certificate	SRA	Stratford Station
EPD	Environmental product declaration	STP	St Pancras Station
EU	European Union	TSB	Technology Strategy Board
EU ETS	European Union Emissions Trading Scheme	UK	United Kingdom
FF&E	Furniture, fixtures and equipment	UKGBC	United Kingdom Green Building Council
FSC	Forest Stewardship Council	US	United States
GAL	Gatwick Airport Limited	USA	Unites States of America
GGBS	Ground granulated blast-furnace slag	VIC	Victoria Station
GHG	Greenhouse gases	WLC	Whole life carbon
GIA	Gross internal (floor) area	WWF	World Wildlife Fund
		WRAP	Waste and Resources Action Programme

IMAGE CREDITS

Chapter 1
p5 SCP with data from Carbon Brief (2015);
p9 RICS Professional Guidance, Global: Methodology to Calculate Embodied Carbon – Lockie (2014);
p9 SCP (Mirko Farnetani, Juan J Lafuente);
p15 SCP (Maiia Guermanova, Pryianka Arora);
p16 CP (Gareth Roberts, Qian Li)

Chapter 2
p17 RIBA Plan of Work 2013 – stages, IBA (2013);
p22 Everyman Theatre, Liverpool. Haworth Tompkins;
p24 Library of Birmingham – SCP (Juan J Lafuente);
p25 "The Shard from the Sky Garden 2015"
    Photo by User: Colin / Wikimedia Commons / CC BY-SA 4.0. 2;
p25 "Cabot Square, Canary Wharf". Photo by David Iliff. License: CC-BY-SA 3.0. 2008;
p27 "Serpentine Pavilion 2016 from gallery"
    Photo by David Hawgood. License: CC BY-SA 2.0. 2016;
p30 Concrete-framed structure in London. HTS;
p31 Heyne Tillett Steel structural engineers;
p33 SCP (Athina Papakosta);
p36 SCP (Mirko Farnetani, Leo Chung, Juan J Lafuente);
p37 SCP (Mirko Farnetani, Leo Chung, Juan J Lafuente);
p38 SCP (Mirko Farnetani);
p39 SCP (Mirko Farnetani, Leo Chung);
p40 © RIBA Collections

Chapter 3
p42 SCP (Mirko Farnetani, Juan J Lafuente);
p46 SCP (Simon Sturgis);
p47 SCP (Simon Sturgis);
p49 SCP (Christina Stuart);
p51 SCP (Christina Stuart);
p52 SCP (Christina Stuart);
p56 SCP (Maiia Guermanova, Pryianka Arora);
p59 Mark Snow SEGRO;
p59 SCP (Gareth Roberts, Qian Li);
p60 SCP (Qian Li);
p62 SCP (Qian Li);
p63 SCP (Simon Sturgis & Qian Li)

Chapter 4
P69 Illustrative heat maps developed for Grosvenor. SCP;
p71 Image courtesy of David Morley Architects;
p71 SCP (Sara Godinho and Athina Papakosta);
p74 SCP (Juan Carlos Vizcaino, Juan Jose Lafuente);
p75 SCP (Juan Carlos Vizcaino, Juan Jose Lafuente);
p76 SCP (Juan Jose Lafuente);
p78 SCP (Juan Jose Lafuente);
p80 SCP (Juan Jose Lafuente);
p81 SCP (Juan Jose Lafuente);
p82 SCP (Juan Jose Lafuente);
p83 SCP (Juan Jose Lafuente);
p86 SCP (Juan Jose Lafuente);
p87 SCP (Juan Jose Lafuente)

Chapter 5
P91 SCP (Gareth Roberts, Maiia Guermanova, Theodore Darviris);
P92 SCP (Gareth Roberts, Maiia Guermanova, Theodore Darviris);
P93 SCP (Gareth Roberts, Maiia Guermanova, Theodore Darviris);
P95 SCP (Gareth Roberts, Maiia Guermanova, Theodore Darviris);
p96 SCP (Juan J Lafuente, Theodore Darviris), with data from Berners-Lee (2010) and 'How Bad are Bananas?' by Mike Berners-Lee;

Chapter 6
p100 BS EN 15978:2011 - BSI (2011A);
p107 SCP (Qian Li);
p108 SCP (Qian Li, Martina Arata);
p109 SCP;
P111 SCP;
P115 SCP (Qian Li, Simon Sturgis);
P116 SCP (Qian Li, Simon Sturgis)

INDEX

CARBON IMPACT OF 1 BOOK OVER A GENERATION

PRINT SPEC				
Finished size	246 x 189	mm	portrait	
Text print	4 colours, both sides			
Text paper type	115	gsm	Arjowiggins Cocoon 100 Silk	100% recycled paper
Cover print	4 pages, 4 colours, one side, biodegradable matt lamination			
Cover paper type	350	gsm	Arjowiggins Cocoon 100 Silk	100% recycled paper
Finish	Fold, perfect bind with drawn on cover and trimmed to size			

PAGES	128		
SHEETS (1 sheet=2 pages)	64		
COVER SHEETS	2		
Total sheet area	2.98	m^2	
Total cover sheet area	0.09	m^2	
Paper weight, per sheet	5.35	g	
Cover weight, per sheet	16.27	g	
Total weight	0.34	kg	pages
	0.03	kg	covers
	0.37	kg	

CARBON CALCULATION				Carbon impact (kgCO$_2$e/kg)	BEIS 2016 Carbon impact (kgCO$_2$e/kg)	
Embodied carbon incl. manufacturing & transport to end users [A1-A4]	660	kgCO$_2$e/t				
	0.66	kgCO$_2$e/kg				
Total embodied carbon	0.23	kgCO$_2$e	pages			
	0.02	kgCO$_2$e	covers			
	0.25	kgCO$_2$e			For comparison / validation only	
End of Life scenarios	Whole Life Carbon			Carbon impact (kgCO$_2$e/kg)	BEIS 2016 Carbon impact (kgCO$_2$e/kg)	
1. Retain	0.25	kgCO$_2$e	Read book and pass on to others/colleagues	0.00	0	
2. Dispose (Landfill)	0.40	kgCO$_2$e	Bin book that will be then sent to landfill	0.42	0.314	
3. Recycle	0.14	kgCO$_2$e	Recycle book	-0.28	0.021	-0.29
			Savings against making a new book from virgin paper		-0.31	-0.29